MODERN WARFARE
THE VIETNAM WAR

Saigon was accustomed to terrorist attacks but the scale of the Tet Offensive came as a complete shock.

MODERN WARFARE

THE VIETNAM WAR

The Tet Offensive 1968

Anthony Tucker-Jones

Pen & Sword
MILITARY

First published in Great Britain in 2014 by
PEN & SWORD MILITARY
an imprint of
Pen & Sword Books Ltd,
47 Church Street,
Barnsley,
South Yorkshire
S70 2AS

ISBN 978 178346 362 6

Typeset by CHIC GRAPHICS

Printed and bound in India by Replika Press Pvt. Ltd.

Pen & Sword Books Ltd incorporates the imprints of Pen & Sword
Archaeology, Atlas, Aviation, Battleground, Discovery, Family History, History,
Maritime, Military, Naval, Politics, Railways, Select, Social History, Transport,
True Crime, and Claymore Press, Frontline Books, Leo Cooper, Praetorian
Press, Remember When, Seaforth Publishing and Wharncliffe.

For a complete list of Pen & Sword titles please contact
Pen & Sword Books Limited
47 Church Street, Barnsley, South Yorkshire S70 2AS, England
E-mail: enquiries@pen-and-sword.co.uk
Website: www.pen-and-sword.co.uk

Contents

Preface

Modern Warfare Series

Pen & Sword's Modern Warfare series is designed to provide a visual account of the defining conflicts of the late twentieth and early twenty-first centuries. These include Operations Desert Storm, Iraqi Freedom and Enduring Freedom. A key characteristic of all three, fought by coalitions, is what has been dubbed 'shock and awe', whereby superior technology, air supremacy and overwhelming firepower ensured complete freedom of manoeuvre on the ground in the face of a numerically stronger enemy. The focus of this series is to explain how military and political goals were achieved so swiftly and decisively.

Another aspect of modern warfare is that it is conducted in the full glare of the international media. This is a trend that first started during the Vietnam War and to this day every aspect of a conflict is visually recorded and scrutinised. Such visual reporting often shapes public perceptions of conflict to a far greater extent than politicians or indeed generals.

All the photos in this book, unless otherwise credited, were issued by the US Department of Defense at the time of the conflict. The author and the publishers are grateful for the work of the various forces' combat photographers.

Introduction

On 30 January 1968 the North Vietnamese communists launched a massive coordinated surprise attack – the Tet Offensive – across South Vietnam against the South Vietnamese and American armies. The world watched in surprise and horror as a superpower was caught off guard and sent reeling. The world's media recorded every key moment as the American military struggled to get a grip on the situation. The fighting was beamed into American homes in glorious colour and there could be no hiding that something had gone drastically wrong with US foreign policy in South-east Asia. Superior firepower and technology eventually crushed the offensive, but it proved to be a major psychological victory for the communists – a turning point in the Vietnam War.

The Tet Offensive, fought at the height of the Vietnam War, was effectively the culmination of America's containment policy, whereby it chose to confront communism wherever it sought to rear its head around the world. Following the Second World War the emergence of the Iron Curtain dividing Europe signalled the start of the Cold War and an armed stand-off with the communist Eastern bloc. The Berlin Airlift and the Cuban Missile Crisis had shown that capitalism and communism could not live hand in hand and twice had brought East and West to the brink of war. In the case of Korea the Cold War went hot after America found itself dragged into a struggle to safeguard South Korea from the communist North and its Chinese allies. The conflict in Vietnam in many ways became a rerun of the Korean War. Washington's worldview was that containment had to be pursued no matter the cost.

During the Tet Offensive Washington was distracted by the Prague Spring crisis which dominated Europe in the first half of 1968. Attempts at liberalising communist rule in Czechoslovakia were met by a massive invasion by Warsaw Pact forces that summer. Fears of a wider nuclear conflict left Western governments impotent, unable to take any action other than vocally condemn the invasion as an act of aggression. Understandably US strategists fretted that the conflict in South-east Asia was a deliberate move by the communist world to distract American military resources from the NATO–Warsaw Pact impasse. At the same time they knew that Moscow's and Beijing's support for communist North Vietnam was a drain on communist resources. Better to fight your enemies far from home than on your very doorstep.

The communist Tet Offensive caught the American military, led by General William C. Westmoreland, off guard with an intelligence failure that ranked alongside that of Pearl Harbor. The North Vietnamese Army (NVA) and Viet Cong (VC) guerrilla assault effectively started in September 1967 when communist forces launched attacks against the isolated American garrisons in the central highlands. With great foresight Westmoreland warned Washington in late December 1967 that he expected the communists 'to undertake an intensified countrywide effort, perhaps a maximum effort, over a relatively short period of time.'

The Vietnamese communists had stepped up their activity by early January 1968 with an attack on Da Nang air base, destroying twenty-seven aircraft. Attacks were also made in the Que Son valley and against the Ban Me Thuot airfield and An Khe. The VC announced a seven-day truce for the Tet holiday, which was scheduled to begin on 28 January, and VC activity died down the day before, apart from shelling of the US base at Khe Sanh.

Nevertheless the South Vietnamese government stated the truce would not be observed in the five northern provinces due to the VC build-up during the past month. Despite such caution they and their American allies were almost overwhelmed by the sheer scale of the Tet Offensive, which saw attacks right across South Vietnam.

In particular the bitter engagement fought at Khe Sanh, in South Vietnam, as part of the Tet assault saw tactical air power coming of age. The American fire support base at Khe Sanh experienced one of the deadliest deluges of munitions unleashed on a tactical target in the history of warfare. Both the siege of Khe Sanh and the bitter battles of Hue and Saigon stretched American resources to breaking point. Although in each case victory was secured, the Tet Offensive was to have far-reaching ramifications for America's commitment to South Vietnam and the conduct of the war.

America's use of the strategy that later became known as 'shock and awe' horrified the American public, many of whom had no stomach for defeating the communists at any price. Despite American ingenuity and technology, the use of overwhelming air power proved to be a blunt instrument that targeted not only enemy soldiers but also innocent civilians. The widespread use of napalm and Agent Orange stripped the US military of any moral authority. Great swathes of Vietnam became a poisoned wasteland.

Tet signalled to the American public that they could not and should not prevail in the Vietnam War – what they demanded of their government was an exit strategy rather than total victory. The US military argued for resources and a second chance. For four long years of guerrilla warfare the communists bided their time before launching another conventional offensive in 1972; when this was stopped in its tracks they waited another three years, by which time American disenchantment with the conflict ensured that they could roll into Saigon largely unopposed.

The lesson America's generals took away from the Tet Offensive and indeed the Vietnam War as a whole was that you needed to achieve complete battlespace dominance on land, in the air and on water to win a war. Despite the array of firepower and technology deployed by America, it could never overcome Vietnam's geography. Cutting the ever-changing Ho Chi Minh trail and securing the vast Mekong Delta and Vietnam's coastline was an impossible task. Likewise, clearing Vietnam's jungles was all but impossible – defoliation was no long-term solution. The country's geography favoured the communists, who were able to manoeuvre around the country despite the best efforts of the US military to dominate the battlefield.

As the French Army discovered during the First Indochina War, taking ground meant holding it and this left bases vulnerable to concerted attack. In contrast the open deserts of Iraq meant that during the Gulf War and subsequent Iraq War the US military had complete battlefield dominance. The war in Afghanistan, however, was more like Vietnam except the jungle was substituted for mountains. The French found in Indochina that scattered strongpoints supported from the air was not a war-winning strategy. It was a mistake that the Americans were to repeat – one that was to ultimately lead to the loss of South Vietnam to communism.

Chapter One

Indochina:
The Gathering Storm

The seeds of the Vietnam War lay in the partition of French colonial Indochine, or Indochina, in the chaos following the end of the Second World War. After France's capitulation in June 1940 the Vichy government in unoccupied southern France, under Marshal Henri-Phillipe Pétain, inadvertently aided Adolf Hitler. Instead of assembling the considerable might of the French Navy and French empire to help oust Hitler, Vichy in a state of disarray spent the next year more concerned about safeguarding its far-flung colonial possessions.

Vichy's policy of 'wait and see' greatly assisted Hitler because unless he could neutralise the powerful French fleet he had no real way of threatening the French empire. This effectively meant the pro-Vichy French military in North Africa and the Near East posed a threat to Britain's vulnerable position in Egypt. For the next two years first Britain and then America were forced to wage war on Vichy.

In the Far East Vichy's stance caused further problems with equally significant ramifications. French forces in Indochina were in no position to resist Japan's demands intended to help the latter in its war against China. Indochina covered a vast area and consisted of five nations: Tonkin, Annam, Cochinchina, Laos and Cambodia. General Catroux agreed to sever the Haipong–Yunnan railway, thereby denying China vital war materials. The Vichy government was furious and removed Catroux. His replacement, Admiral Decoux, soon found himself barraged with further Japanese demands, including freedom to move Japanese troops within Indochina and access to French air bases and naval facilities.

Vichy recognised Japan as the pre-eminent power in the region under the Franco-Japanese treaty of 30 August 1940 and acquiesced to Japanese pressure. Orders did not reach Decoux in time to prevent units of the French Foreign Legion resisting the Japanese in Tonkin at Lang Son, not far from the Chinese border. The French lost 800 troops before the Japanese moved on Haipong, and Decoux was finally forced to agree to the presence of Japanese troops.

Ironically Vichy France ensured America's entry into the war. In July 1941 America and Britain demanded the withdrawal of Japanese troops from Indochina and instigated an oil embargo. Japan's response was to attack British and America interests in the Pacific, most notably Pearl Harbor. However, the stretched Japanese military waited until March 1945 to take over Indochina completely.

Five months later the city of Hanoi fell to the communist Viet Minh forces on 19 August 1945 and their leader Ho Chi Minh declared the foundation of the Democratic Republic of Vietnam, appointing General Vo Nguyen Giap as his interior minister. It is doubtful that Minh actually believed the French would give up Indochina so easily, but at least he had affirmed that the Vietnamese wanted independence. Although France recognised the new republic it was reluctant to relinquish control of the abundant rice and rubber plantations in the south. While the French mounted operations in Cochinchina, Cambodia and southern Annam to subdue the communists and other armed groups, they attempted to reach an agreement with the Viet Minh in the north. Exhausted by the Second World War the last thing France needed was a major war on its hands. Giap took to the Tonkinese Mountains, from where his 60,000 guerrillas waged a hit-and-run campaign in late 1946 against the French military and commercial interests.

The fighting rapidly escalated once China and the Soviet Union recognised the Democratic Republic of Vietnam in 1950 and the Viet Minh began to receive significant quantities of Chinese and Soviet weapons. By early 1953 the Viet Minh numbered at least 139,000 men, including 125,000 regulars. Although the French and their local allies had a three-to-one numerical superiority the bulk of their forces were tied down holding strongpoints and the major cities. In Tonkin and in parts of neighbouring Laos the Viet Minh had taken the initiative.

French reliance on fortified 'hedgehogs' (or mutually supporting strongpoints) meant that aircraft played an increasingly important role. The French Air Force deployed 300 aircraft to Vietnam while the French Navy operated three aircraft carriers from the China Sea. This reliance on strongpoints re-supplied by air was a flawed strategy – one that the Americans would repeat during the Second Indochina War.

Vietnam was partitioned by a demilitarised zone (DMZ) in 1954 between the communist north (comprising Tonkin and the northern half of Annam) and the non-communist south (comprising Cochchina and the southern half of Annam). That year the French were decisively defeated at Dien Bien Phu. They could have continued the war but General Giap's victory was such that France lost the will to continue the struggle against communism in South-east Asia.

American President Harry Truman first dispatched the US Military Assistance Advisory Group (MAAG) to Vietnam to assist the French in the First Indochina War in September 1950. MAAG's role was to supervise $10 million worth of US military equipment sent to aid the French in their efforts against the Viet Minh forces. This aid increased dramatically to $350 million in 1953 to replace old French military equipment. Nevertheless, it was not until 1954 that General Henri Navarre, the commanding general of French forces in Indochina, permitted the US to send liaison officers to Vietnamese forces, but by then the writing was already on the wall for France's hold on South Vietnam.

Between 1950 and 1954 America provided $1.1 billion of aid to help France with the war against communism in Indochina, including $746 million worth of equipment delivered direct to the French Expeditionary Force (FEF). It was not enough to help stem the tide. The dramatic and decisive battle of Dien Bien Phu had opened with a French paratroop drop on the Viet-Minh-held village in 1953. It was one of three sites that the French hoped to use to pin down the communist interior. The garrison of 16,000 men, comprising French, Algerians, Moroccans, Thais, Vietnamese and Montagnards, found themselves besieged by 50,000 communist troops.

The defenders endured a bombardment of about 150,000 shells during March–May 1954. All their supplies had to be flown in from Hanoi 300km away. They held out for eight grim weeks in the most appalling conditions until finally forced to surrender. The humiliated French lost 2,293 killed, 5,134 wounded and 11,000 POWs (including wounded) – at a cost of 8,000 dead and 15,000 wounded communists. It was a military disaster for the French and the inevitable recriminations undermined the French government of Indochina.

Crucially, air support had been insufficient: as a result the garrison had been denied reinforcements and prevented from breaking out. The weak French air bridge lost sixty-two aircraft with another 167 damaged. The French defeat had all the hallmarks of Stalingrad in 1943 and it was a lesson the North Vietnamese and Americans were not to forget.

Afterwards the Geneva Accords of July 1954 established two Vietnamese states separated by the Ben Hai River at the 17th Parallel. This ended French combat operations. A demilitarised zone was created along the line of the river and French troops withdrew from the North and the Viet Minh from the South. Cambodia and Laos became independent countries. This finally brought to an end the Union Française that had been created in 1949 to hold France's colonial interests together.

By 1955 the FEF had been reduced to 35,000, with the withdrawal from the country accelerating the following year to coincide with elections throughout Vietnam, which were to unify the country under an independent government. By this time the French had much more pressing matters in Algeria. South Vietnam, alarmed at the prospect of the communists taking power, rejected the elections and disputed the Geneva Accords. This sowed the seeds for the Second Indochina War.

Determined to see the two halves of the country united, the South's Viet Cong or Vietnamese Communists (VC) began a terrorist campaign in the late 1950s. In 1960 the VC were incorporated into the National Liberation Front (NLF), which called for a sustained guerrilla war, rather than a North Korean-style conventional war, to forcibly unite the country.

In late 1945 the French Expeditionary Force sought to reoccupy the former colony of Indochina, consisting of Tonkin in the north, Annam and Cochinchina in the south and Cambodia and Laos. The standard tank of the FEF was the American-supplied M5A1 – this was superseded, thanks to the US military aid programme, by the M24 Chaffee (seen here) from 1950 onwards and it remained in service throughout the First Indochina War.

A French machine-gun team photographed in Indochina in the summer of 1951. They are manning a US-supplied Browning .30-calibre machine gun.

The Indochinese nationalist/communist forces operating against the Japanese during the Second World War were supplied by the Americans. They were then armed with Soviet, Chinese, East European and captured US and French weapons.

French troops arriving at Phong Savan after the Viet Minh retreat in mid-May 1953. The following year the French were decisively defeated at Dien Bien Phu.

Communist Vietnamese troops – some 50,000 were gathered for the siege of Dien Bien Phu.

French M24 Chaffees firing on communist positions. When Second World War veteran General de Lattre de Tassigny took charge in the early 1950s French armoured units were reorganised, with the M24 equipping both the armoured groups and the reconnaissance groups.

The French airlifted ten M24s to Dien Bien Phu to bolster their positions during the fifty-five-day siege. Although the French were generally better equipped than the guerrillas they were outgunned and outnumbered during the battle that lasted from 1 March to 8 May 1954.

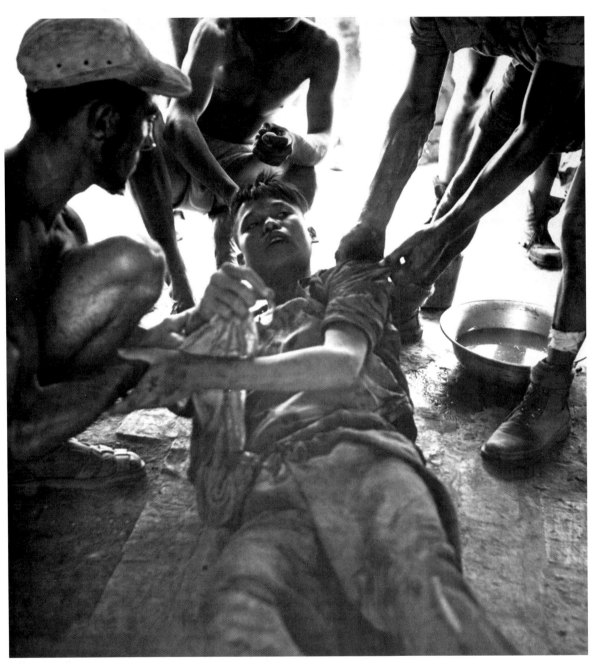

A wounded Vietnamese colonial soldier getting medical treatment. The French garrison at Dien Bien Phu included Vietnamese, Algerian, Montagnard, Moroccan and Thai colonial troops.

French positions at Dien Bien Phu. The surrender was a humiliation: on 7 May General Christian de Castries and 11,000 men surrendered; the rest of the garrison to the south followed suit twenty-four hours later.

Viet Minh troops celebrating. The Geneva Agreements of 1954 deprived France of its South-east Asian colonies. While the diplomatic negotiations were going on, at Dien Bien Phu the Viet Minh dashed French hopes of maintaining a hold in the region.

The Geneva conference agreed to a ceasefire line along the 17th Parallel (later the demilitarised zone) with a 300-day period of free movement across the line for Vietnamese pro- and anti-communist forces. This photo shows French sailors helping refugees board a US naval vessel for the journey south.

Vietnamese refugees boarding *LST 516* at Haipong for their journey to Saigon. Under Operation Passage to Freedom in October 1954 the US navy moved 293,000 people from the newly created North Vietnam to South Vietnam.

US special forces in the Vietnamese jungle initially acted as advisers. Following the Geneva settlement Ho Chi Minh spent his time consolidating power in the north. Le Duan, the senior Viet Minh leader, remained in the south and by 1957 was urging a renewal of the guerrilla war. Alarmed by communist attacks on Laos and South Vietnam, US forces arrived in late 1961 to support President Ngo Dinh Diem.

A USAF 36th Tactical Fighter Squadron Republic F-105D Thunderchief being loaded with Mk 82 500lb bombs at Korat Royal Thai Air Force Base, Thailand in 1964.

The US aircraft carrier USS *Constellation* with the Attack Carrier Air Wing 14 deployed to Vietnam during May 1964–February 1965.

USS *Hancock* was one of the first American carriers 'on line' following the 1964 Tonkin incident when North Vietnamese motor torpedo boats attacked the US destroyer USS *Maddox*.

USAF F-105 'Thuds' poised to take off on a bombing mission over North Vietnam in 1966.

As the war progressed increasing numbers of US ground troops were committed to the war in Vietnam.

In the South Vietnamese capital of Saigon, Viet Cong blew up the Brinks hotel on 24 December 1964, killing two American advisers and injuring fifty-one Americans and Vietnamese. This was one of the Viet Cong's most spectacular acts of terrorism. The following year US Marines came ashore at Da Nang.

The carriers *Hancock, Coral Sea* and *Ranger* air wings were involved in a 100-aircraft strike against the Chanh Hoa barracks in North Vietnam in February 1965 in retaliation for Viet Cong attacks against US facilities in South Vietnam. These retaliatory Flaming Dart missions were quickly replaced by the sustained Rolling Thunder attacks.

US Marines from the 1st Battalion, 3rd Marine Division arriving at Da Nang airbase on 8 March 1965; they were airlifted from Okinawa by USAF C-130 Hercules transport aircraft.

US patrol boats guarding against Vietnamese fishing junks gun running. While the North Vietnamese infiltration route along the Ho Chi Minh trail south through Laos and Cambodia and the Sihanouk trail north through Cambodia were a major security headache, so were the vast waterways of the Mekong Delta. Around 50,000 junks plied their trade along the Mekong River and neighbouring coastal waterways.

Four Douglas two-seater A-1E Skyraider ground-attack aircraft in formation over South Vietnam en route to their target on 25 June 1965. The aircraft were assigned to the 34th Tactical Group based at Bien Hoa, South Vietnam. In US Navy service single-seat A-1Hs and A-1Js played a part in the early offensive against the North but were replaced by A-6s on the large carriers and A-4s and A-7s on the smaller carriers. The single-seaters and the two-seat A-1Es and A-1Gs saw considerable service with USAF's Air Commando squadrons attacking the Ho Chi Minh trail and escorting rescue helicopters.

Chapter Two

Strategic Intelligence Blunder

By the late 1960s and the eve of the Tet Offensive the US Military Assistance Command Vietnam (MACV) and the Central Intelligence Agency (CIA) were at bitter loggerheads over enemy numbers in the south – with estimates ranging from 300,000 to 430,000 respectively. MACV argued local Viet Cong (VC) guerrillas should not be included – only North Vietnamese Army (NVA) infiltrators; the CIA was aghast as the VC were responsible for half of all American casualties.

American intelligence by late 1967 indicated that four NVA infantry divisions with two artillery regiments and supporting armour, totalling 40,000 men, were moving toward the American base at Khe Sanh in the northernmost Quang Tri province. Notably the Tet truce did not encompass I Corps, whose area of responsibility included the northern provinces of South Vietnam.

South Vietnamese intelligence estimated communist forces at 323,000 (including 130,000 regulars and 160,000 guerrillas); in contrast the CIA and US State Department put the figure as high as half a million. Thanks to China and the Soviet Union weapons were not a problem for the communists either. This suggested that the enemy had the upper hand from the very start.

General Joseph McChristian, MACV's intelligence chief, argued inclusion of the VC in the assessment 'would create a political bombshell', as it clearly indicated that the communists 'had the capability and the will to continue a protracted war of attrition.' In layman's terms it meant America was losing the fight before it had even started.

Nonetheless, by the end of 1967 Washington claimed that it was winning the war of attrition, having declared NVA/VC losses at 165,000 men (88,000 killed in action, 30,000 dead or disabled from wounds, 6,000 POWs, 18,000 defectors and 25,000 lost to desertion and disease). On the ground things were very different: official intelligence reports of NVA/VC strength in South Vietnam were in fact double those released to the public.

On the basis of heavy communist losses General Westmoreland was claiming publicly they were 'unable to mount a major offensive . . . I am absolutely certain that whereas in 1965 the enemy was winning, today he is certainly losing . . . We have reached an important point when the end begins to come into view.' In light of the available intelligence, his later show of bravado – 'I hope they try something, because we are looking for a fight' – was ill-founded.

Meanwhile Giap and his fellow generals felt that the time was ripe to repeat the Dien Bien Phu strategy and deliver a body blow to America's resolution to prop up the hated South. Rifts in the American government and the growing peace movement only served to encourage him. Certainly Giap's Chief of Staff General Van Tien Dung and Ho Chi Minh's right-hand man, politician Le Duan, were spoiling for a fight. NVA General Tran Van Tra's sights were set on Saigon and General Tran Do's on the key city of Hue.

As predicted, the communists stepped up their activity by early January 1968 with an attack on Da Nang air base. Attacks were also made in the Que Son valley and against the Ban Me Thuot airfield and An Khe. However, the seven-day truce for the Tet lunar holiday was scheduled to begin on 28 January and activity died down the day before, apart from shelling of the American base at Khe Sanh. Nevertheless, the South Vietnamese government refused to observe the ceasefire in its five northern provinces due to the ongoing communist military build-up.

Khe Sanh, a few miles from the Laotian border in the western half of Quang Tri, had been a US special forces camp until 3,500 US marines arrived in 1967. The Green Berets then moved to the Montagnard village of Lang Vei, closer to the Laotian border to the south-west. Khe Sanh – straddling Route 9, an old French road linking Dong Ha on the coast with Laotian towns along the Mekong – was then expanded to act as a springboard for proposed operations against communist bases in Laos and the bordering DMZ. Its defences were built around the vital airstrip and three hills to the north-west (881 North, 881 South and 861A). A detachment was also on Hill 950 to the north on the other side of the Rao Quan River.

The US 3rd Marine Regiment secured the hills during the spring of 1967 after prematurely triggering an attack from the north-west. They lost 155 killed and 425 wounded, whilst the NVA lost 940 men. More importantly the battle cost the NVA control of the vital ground overlooking Khe Sanh and the forces that had been gathered for the attack on the base itself. Fighting during July–October resulted in another 113 NVA fatalities for the loss of ten marines. The 3rd Marines were then rotated out and replaced by the 26th Marines.

Despite the ongoing fighting, the base had no overall strategic significance and little tactical value. Its main function was to monitor the Ho Chi Minh trail across the border, down which communist weapons poured, and disrupt it with artillery fire. If the base came under attack or was encircled it would not be able to carry out this role. The Americans could simply interdict the trail from elsewhere. The site was also difficult to defend as security relied on holding the hills, while the water supply passed through enemy territory.

The marines wanted to leave, but General Westmoreland was of a different opinion. He no doubt felt it would be unwise for American troops to give ground in the face of a conventional rather than guerrilla NVA/VC attack. Westmoreland wanted to fight a conventional battle and was adamant there would be no repeat of Dien Bien Phu. Furthermore as enemy action was expected over the Tet holiday MACV felt it prudent to counter it in an area where it was most anticipated, thereby tying down communist forces and preventing them from causing mischief elsewhere. Whatever the case, the marines were ordered to stay and fight, largely for symbolic reasons. This decision also left the isolated garrison at Lang Vei to its fate.

In contrast Khe Sanh was of vital importance to the NVA/VC in the north-west corner of South Vietnam, just fourteen miles from the DMZ and six miles from the Laotian section of the Ho Chi Minh trail. Its shelling of the trail was a major nuisance and its capture would ease logistical problems and be a morale booster. The communists would be easily able to sustain an attack and their long-range artillery could operate from the safety of the DMZ. Ironically Giap's strategic plans ran on similar lines to MACV's but in reverse: Khe Sanh was to direct attention away from a major offensive which the communists were planning for the whole of South Vietnam.

Just three days after Washington called a halt to the bombing of the North's capital Hanoi and six days after the halt to the bombing of Haiphong (North Vietnam's main port) in preparation for the Tet holiday truce, the North struck at Khe Sanh. The communists allowed themselves only ten days before the more general offensive so they had to act quickly. General Giap's strategy was to take the surrounding hills and then use them as artillery positions to seal the airstrip. The American forces at Lang Vei were to be cut off and destroyed while Khe Sanh would first be worn down and then overrun. Giap's major failing was to underestimate Westmoreland's ability to resupply his forces by air: in effect it would prove almost impossible to cut the garrison off completely.

A marine patrol bumped into NVA forces on 17 January 1968 south-west of Hill 881N. Over the next few days contact with the enemy continued. A prisoner from the North Vietnamese 325C Division informed the marines that the NVA were planning attacks on Hills 881S and 861. This was to be followed by a thrust from the east, with diversionary attacks from the northern and western sectors. The main attack was to be conducted by the 304th Division, which, using the woods as cover, was to seize the airstrip. Both sides knew that without the airstrip resistance would quickly crumble. Late on the 20th, 300 NVA attacked Hill 861 as predicted, but their reserves were pinned down by American artillery fire and the assault repulsed. The attack on Hill 881S never materialised.

In the early hours of 21 January Khe Sanh base received its first bombardment; in the shelling eighteen Americans were killed and forty wounded, the main supply dump was blown up, with 1,300 tons of precious ammunition, a helicopter was wrecked and five others damaged. Probing attacks were also launched against the marine garrisons holding the hills and against Lang Vei. At Khe Sanh village the defenders endured two attacks by the 304th Division; the next day they were forced back into the base compound. The marine commander at Khe Sanh base, Colonel David Lownds, had some of the villagers and local Vietnamese civilians flown to Da Nang and Quang Tri. Nevertheless, about 6,000 refugees had to be excluded from the base during the course of the battle. He also tried to keep the road open with Lang Vei.

Westmoreland's response was swift: a supporting air campaign dubbed Operation Niagara was implemented. Khe Sanh received 1,500 reinforcements, boosting the garrison to over 5,000, and USAF planes and army helicopters flew in supplies. A fresh battalion of marines was deployed and some two-thirds of the infantry were placed on the hills, including about thirty men on Hill 950 and about 400 men on Hill 558. The rest were used for perimeter defence of the base itself, supported by artillery, mortars and five M48 tanks. Giap now had a major battle on his hands.

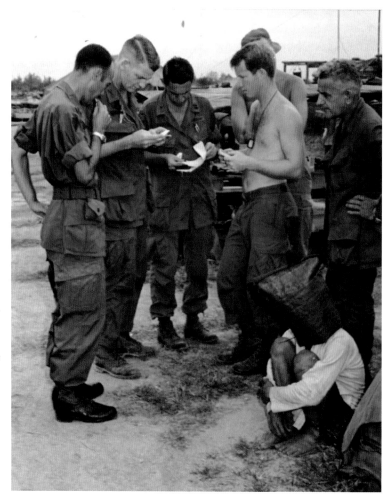

US troops interrogating a suspected Viet Cong – while intelligence indicated that the North Vietnamese Army and Viet Cong were planning something for the Tet holiday, they had no idea of its scale.

Two views across the 10km-wide demilitarised zone to North Vietnam in March 1968. The Ben Hai River and the 17th Parallel became the dividing line with the partitioning of Vietnam in July 1954. The water-filled craters testify to the intensity of shelling this area endured.

Yet more VC prisoners – by the end of 1967 US forces claimed that they had taken 6,000 prisoners. One of the earliest helicopters deployed to South-east Asia was the Sikorsky UH-34, which was used by the US Army, Navy and Marine Corps as well as South Vietnamese forces. This one belongs to the marine medium transport squadron HMM-161 and was photographed during Operation Starlight south of Chu Lai on 1 August 1965; note the M60 door gun.

This Viet Cong was killed in the grounds of the US embassy in Saigon on 31 January 1968 during the Tet Offensive. By the end of the previous year NVA/VC forces were assessed to have lost 88,000 men in action.

American ground-attack aircraft did not have it all their own way.

M113 armoured personnel carriers – initially the American high command deemed South-east Asia unsuitable for armoured warfare. Originally seen as a 'combat taxi', the M113 soon developed into a assault vehicle and over 40,000 saw service in Vietnam.

General Westmoreland accompanying President Johnson on a visit to South Vietnam to assess the US presence.

Publicly America was claiming that it was winning the war in South Vietnam by 1968 – but behind the scenes the CIA and the US Military Advisory Command Vietnam were at loggerheads over the size of communist forces.

A 'tunnel rat' from the 1st Battalion, 5th Infantry Regiment, US 25th Infantry Division about to investigate a VC underground bunker complex during Operation Cedar Knolls in Binh Duong province in 1967.

An Australian soldier examining a VC tunnel during Operation Crimp in 1966. Australian advisers arrived in Vietnam from 1962 onwards and over 7,000 Australians and New Zealanders were deployed by 1969.

Another shot taken during Operation Crimp. This Australian taking a break in VC living quarters gives a good indication of how sophisticated underground communist facilities could be.

MACV's HQ at Tan Son Nhut: one of the targets of the communist Tet Offensive.

US rangers in their distinctive tiger-stripe camouflage call in an air strike – the man in the background is equipped with the M16 assault rifle. Tiger stripe was also used by US special forces and some ARVN units such as the rangers.

To patrol South Vietnam's waterways the US navy set up Task Force 116, the River Patrol Force, in 1965. Codenamed Game Warden the US forces were supplied with about 425 river patrol boats. However, the veterans of riverine warfare preferred the slower but heavily armoured landing craft that were converted into river monitors. This particular fast patrol craft PCF-38 belonged to Coastal Division 11.

US Navy SEALs on the Bassac River south of Saigon in 1967.

US perimeter guards armed with the M14 rifle. At Tan Son Nhut air base security was far from adequate in 1968. The M14 replaced the venerable M1 Garand of Second World War fame and had been in service since the end of the Korean War. All the men are wearing body army or armoured vests, generally known as flak jackets – in marine service this was the M1955: weighing 10lb, it consisted of twenty-two overlapping fibreglass plates.

A Douglas A-1E, with Pave Pat bombs, at Nakhom Phanom Royal Thai Air Force Base on 29 September 1968.

On a mission over North Vietnam this US Navy Douglas A-4E Skyhawk packs a punch with six Mk 82 500lb bombs and two AGM-12 Bullpup missiles. The aircraft is from attack squadron VA-164 Ghost Riders, which deployed to Vietnam from 16 June 1967 to 31 January 1968 on the carrier USS *Oriskany* as part of Carrier Air Wing 16.

Chapter Three

ARVN:
Too Little Too Late

The army of South Vietnam consisted of a collection of former French colonial units. With American help it slowly improved, gaining some counter-insurgency capabilities, but political upheaval undermined it. Newly elected president, John F. Kennedy, agreed with MAAG's requests for increases to the Army of the Republic of Vietnam's (ARVN) troop levels and the US military commitment in both equipment and men. In response, Kennedy provided $28.4 million in funding for the ARVN, and overall military aid increased from $50 million per year to $144 million in 1961. This set the tone for America's ever-growing military commitment to South Vietnam.

The Buddhist uprising and the fall of the government in 1963 led to the deterioration of the South Vietnamese armed forces and only the intervention of US combat forces saved the republic. American military advisers, who became designated the US Military Assistance Command Vietnam (MACV), began to arrive in the early 1960s, with the first combat troops arriving in 1965, followed by Australian and New Zealand forces. South Korea and Thailand were also to provide men. The North responded by committing regulars of the North Vietnamese Army (NVA). Between 1965 and 1968 American forces were to bear the brunt of the fighting.

MACV came into being on 8 February 1962 as a result of the increased US military presence in South Vietnam. It was initially tasked with assisting the US Military Assistance Advisory Group (MAAG) Vietnam, controlling every advisory and assistance effort in Vietnam. As this task expanded, on 15 May 1964 MACV's role was extended and it absorbed MAAG Vietnam when combat unit deployment became too large for advisory group control.

Initially MACV directed naval operations as well but on 1 April 1966, Naval Forces, Vietnam was created to command the naval units in the II, III and IV Corps' tactical zones. This eventually included the major combat formations of the Coastal Surveillance Force (Task Force 115), River Patrol Force (Task Force 116) and Riverine Assault Force (Task Force 117). MACV continued directing US military operations in Vietnam until 29 March 1973 when the Paris Peace Accords agreed to the withdrawal of all foreign troops from Vietnam.

America's strategy was to set up fortified bases along the coast (Phu Bai, Da Nang, Chui Lai, Qui Nhon and Cam Rahn) from which to conduct operations. There were to be no frontlines except around the main bases, meaning that the countryside was left to the mercy of the VC. The Americans' primary goal was to cut the Ho Chi Minh trail, down which the North supplied the communist forces operating in the South. Air power was chosen as the instrument to achieve this.

Despite American dollars, by 1968 the general condition of the South Vietnamese armed forces (SVAF) can only have encouraged the communists. In 1954–5 SVAF numbers stood at 279,000; by 1968 they had almost tripled to 820,000 – the ARVN had grown from 170,000 to 380,000. However, in 1967 the ARVN had been relegated to a secondary role: pacification and security operations. The large-scale US involvement precluded equipment modernisation for the ARVN until after 1968. This was to have far-reaching ramifications for the US military. Furthermore, absenteeism and desertion from the ARVN was a major problem and large numbers of men were missing at the start of Tet.

Desertions for the whole of 1968 numbered 139,670 and were the largest single cause of manpower loss in South Vietnam. Desertion from the SVAF had risen from 73,000 in 1964 to 113,000 in 1965. In an effort to counter this, General Westmoreland ordered American units to adopt certain ARVN forces. After some improvement the rate rose from 10.5 per 1,000 in 1967 to 16.5 by July 1968, amounting to some 13,000 desertions, the highest monthly rate since 1966, before reaching an all-time high in October 1968 with 17.2 per 1,000. The apathetic attitude ended sharply with Tet and clearly the ARVN should have been given a greater share of the fighting between 1965 and 1968.

Furthermore, the ARVN was weak in armour. It established its first armoured units in 1956, equipped with Second World War vintage American vehicles (such as the M24 Chaffee, M8 armoured car and M3 half-track) abandoned by the French. Six years later two mechanised companies were formed using the M113 armoured personnel carrier (APC), which saw service for the first time on 11 June 1962 in the Mekong Delta. The ARVN was soon to learn that the M113 was not just an armoured bus but also an effective armoured fighting vehicle in its own right.

The ARVN's old Chaffees were replaced by the M41A3 Walker Bulldog light tank in 1965 and its forces expanded to eight armoured cavalry regiments, equipped with the M41A3, M113, M8 and M106 (self-propelled 4.2-inch mortar). During the Tet Offensive ten ARVN armoured cavalry regiments fought to contain the communist insurgents.

Ironically just two days before the Tet Offensive the US National Security Council held discussions on how to 'de-Americanise' the war. It was optimistically felt that the ARVN was almost at the point where this could happen. To facilitate this process it was decided that a 'Vietnamisation' programme would be instigated to strengthen the ARVN further and extend the pacification programme in South Vietnam. The problem with this was that the ARVN needed to greatly improve its mobility, which meant training more helicopter pilots, but this took time. Such plans had to be swiftly shelved in the face of Tet.

While the ARVN was hardly in an ideal condition to face the coming storm in 1968, South Vietnam's air force was not in a much better position. The Vietnamese Air Force, or VNAF, came into being in the mid-1950s, equipped with F8F Bearcat aircraft supplied by the French. Once America openly intervened, VNAF was rapidly overshadowed by the USAF. Initially the Americans supplied T-28 Trojan trainers and H-19 and H-34 helicopters, which American pilots often secretly flew. In 1965 the first jets arrived, in the shape of B-57 Canberra bombers as well as the UH-1 helicopter. These were followed by A-1 Skyraider and A-37 Dragonfly light attack aircraft as well as the F-5 Freedom Fighter – on the whole, though, the VNAF was confined to a counter-insurgency role; it was the USAF that took the bomber war to North Vietnam.

In February 1968 the VNAF's strength stood at 16,277 personnel, organised into seventeen squadrons equipped with 362 aircraft. The Vietnamese B-57 programme had been aborted in early 1966 after a number of accidents. Instead, in June 1967 F-5s manned by VNAF combat veterans went operational with the 522nd Fighter Squadron, which by early 1968 was managing almost 700 sorties per month. The VNAF also had the 514th, 516th, 518th, 520th and 524th fighter squadrons flying the propeller-driven A-1Hs and A-1Gs, a version of the Skyraider fitted with dual controls and used by USAF pilots to provide combat training to new VNAF pilots.

On the very eve of Tet the VNAF strike force consisted of seventeen F-5A/Bs stationed at Bien Hoa and sixty-nine A-1G/Hs at Bien Hoa, Binh Thuy, Da Nang and Nha Trang. When the offensive opened on 30 January 60 per cent of the VNAF's personnel were on leave for the Lunar New Year. Likewise the conversion of VNAF units – led by the 524th Fighter Squadron, which had stood down at Nha Trang in January 1968 – to the Cessna A-37B was temporarily interrupted by the Tet Offensive as all available pilots were thrown straight into battle. As a result deliveries of the A-37Bs were made in November 1968, with the 524th Fighter Squadron only becoming operational with this aircraft the following year, followed by the 520th and 516th squadrons.

The VNAF in 1968 was very weak in transport aircraft and helicopters; it was also operating much older airframes than the USAF and the Australian Air Force. At the start of the year its three helicopter squadrons were not up to strength (a fourth had been abandoned); this was only achieved in March 1968 with the arrival of a final batch of H-34 helicopters. The modernisation of the VNAF's transport fleet, which consisted of three squadrons of C-47s, only started in March 1968 with the conversion of the 413th Transport Squadron to Fairchild C-119Gs.

Initially communist forces in Vietnam and indeed Cambodia and Laos relied upon captured French weapons. Although some standardisation was achieved in the later stages of the war, there was still a huge amount of variety in communist small arms. The one weapon that was very common and became an icon of the conflict was the AK-47 in its many guises. Soviet, Chinese and Czech assault rifles were all supplied in great quantity. The Soviet SKS or Chicom Type 56 semi-automatic rifle was likewise widely used by the NVA and later by the Viet Cong.

Soviet and Chinese aid to North Vietnam by 1964 amounted to $800 million, most of it in the form of military equipment, the majority of which was Soviet. The Chinese supplied the Vietnamese communists with small arms while the Soviets provided support weapons such as artillery and, more importantly, surface-to-air missiles (SAMs). In particular sufficient quantities of the Kalashnikov AK-47 assault rifle were received by the North for them to be shipped clandestinely to South Vietnam and used to equip most of the Viet Cong guerrilla units. This partially alleviated the headache of trying to cope with so many different types of small arms and the logistical problems they created.

By 1968 most Viet Cong and the North Vietnamese Army units were predominantly equipped with the Chinese copy of the AK-47, the Type 56 identifiable by the fitted triangular bayonet and the Type 56-1 folding-stock assault rifle. They also used the Type 50, the Chinese copy of the Soviet PPSh-41 and the VC produced their own version, known as the K-50M, in their jungle workshops. Subsequently these weapons were supplied to the communist Khmer Rouge guerrillas in Cambodia and the Pathet Lao in Laos.

ARVN M113. In April 1962 ARVN formed two mechanised companies, each with fifteen M113 armoured personnel carriers, and on 11 June 1962 they were deployed operationally for the first time in the Mekong Delta. Initially they were used as little more than armoured buses but were soon employed as armoured fighting vehicles.

ARVN recruits wearing the standard Olive Green 107 fatigues and the M1 steel helmet . The men in the lower two photos have been issued with the M16 and the man in the upper has the much older M1 Garand.

These ARVN troops have a mixture of camouflage pattern types: the man at the front has tiger stripes while the one in the middle is wearing leaf pattern utilities. The latter were favoured by the Hac Bao or Black Panthers of the ARVN 1st Division's strike company which saw action in Hue in 1968. ARVN rangers generally wore a tiger-stripe variant; the Vietnamese also produced their own copies, which the Americans called 'duck-hunter pattern'. ARVN rangers from the 30th or 38th Battalion wore the duck-hunter pattern in Saigon in 1968.

VNAF transport aircraft.

In the early 1960s US special forces began training ARVN ranger and paratroop units.

Cessna A-37Bs belonging to the 520th Tactical Fighter Squadron, 74th Tactical Fighter Wing, South Vietnamese Air Force. Thanks to the Vietnamisation programme the A-37Bs became the most numerous combat aircraft in the VNAF fleet.

During 1965 the ARVN's old M24 Chaffees were replaced by M41A3 light tanks.

Two more ARVN soldiers in OGs. By 1968 desertion was a major problem for the ARVN.

Members of the Viet Cong main force or North Vietnamese Army armed with Mosin-Nagant bolt-action carbines. The standard NVA uniform was a dark-green or tan-khaki cotton shirt and trousers and the famous sun helmet made of cardboard impregnated with resin. They also wore a floppy bush hat which came in a variety of colours. In the second image they are taking instruction on the Soviet-supplied RPD light machine gun.

A US soldier examining a captured AK-47 assault rifle.

Members of the NVA armed with the ubiquitous AK-47 assault rifle photographed in 1965.

ARVN Biet Dong Quan or rangers in action in Saigon in 1968. The third man in is armed with the American M79 'blooper' grenade launcher. The 6.2lb M79 could fire between five and seven 40mm grenade rounds per minute to a range of 430 yards. It was a light indirect-fire weapon that proved particularly effective in close terrain.

US engineers preparing to destroy a VC tunnel complex.

US special forces were also instrumental with the Civilian Irregular Defense Group programme which trained local minority groups to protect themselves from the VC. These 'Cidgees' units gave rise to mobile strike forces and by 1968 there were thirty-four Mobile Strike Force Command (MIKE Force) companies.

Skyraider of the VNAF 516th Fighter Squadron being loaded with napalm at Da Nang air base in May 1967. The VNAF received its first AD-6s (A-1Hs) in 1960 and operated both single-seat and two-seat versions of the Skyraider until 1975. Large numbers of Skyraiders were transfered to the VNAF and France also supplied Cambodia with fifteen AD-4Nas (A-1Ds).

Chapter Four

Rolling Thunder

Despite many of its personnel being on leave for Tet, the VNAF reacted swiftly, with those aircrews on duty bearing the brunt of the opening air operations until their comrades returned. The VNAF got as many aircraft into the air as possible, throwing a lifeline to hard-pressed ARVN units on the ground. During late January this included 215 sorties by fighter aircraft, 196 by reconnaissance aircraft, 158 by transport aircraft and 215 by helicopters. During February these sortie rates increased, with the VNAF strafing and bombing NVA/VC forces throughout the country.

One of the new aircraft types that joined the fighting over South Vietnam in 1968 was the twin-turbo-prop OV-10A Bronco, which deployed to Bien Hoa in late July. The first OV-10As assigned to the forward-air-controller (FAC) role served with the USAF's 504th Tactical Air Support Group, which had lost four O-1s and four O-2s during the battle for Hue.

The USAF, USN and the VNAF conducted an escalating bombing campaign against North Vietnamese targets under the codename Operation Rolling Thunder from 2 March 1965 to 2 November 1968. While this was the largest air offensive conducted since the Second World War, it was greatly hampered by inter-service rivalry and political restraints. In addition the USAF was woefully ill-prepared for this type of operation, having spent decades planning for nuclear war against the Soviet Union. In contrast the USN had the new A-6 Intruder all-weather fighter bomber and was responsible for the F-4 Phantom, which became ubiquitous during the Vietnam War.

In part Rolling Thunder was intended to deter Hanoi from supporting the war in the south by cutting its supply routes, along which flowed equipment and men. Instead North Vietnam greatly strengthened its air defences, taking a deadly toll on its attackers and continued to supply the NVA/VC. There was also a hope that the air attacks would force Hanoi to the negotiating table.

The Tet Offensive was a nasty wake-up call for the USAF, USN and the VNAF that showed their efforts had been largely for nothing. In early 1968 all available aircraft were diverted to support Operation Niagara during the siege of Khe Sanh. Likewise the B-52 tactical bombing raids, known as Operation Arc Light, were also deployed in support of the US marines at Khe Sanh.

Vietnam saw one of the most intensive air wars fought over a ten-year period.

No other air war – with the exception of Korea – has come anywhere close to the massive number of sorties conducted by the United States Air Force over Vietnam. Here the F-4 Phantom assumed the mantle of the P-51 Mustang of the Second World War and the Sabre of Korea. It accounted for 107 enemy fighter aircraft (and one kill shared with an F-105). During 1965–7 four MiGs were shot down for every American fighter lost. However, the Americans were nowhere near the ten-to-one ratio established during the Korean War.

At the height of US involvement a daily average of 800 sorties were flown by US fighter bombers in support of the ground forces. In a single year four American aircraft types alone flew well over 80,000 sorties. The USAF dropped over six million tons of ordnance in South-east Asia, more than double that used in the Second World War and Korea combined. During the war the North Vietnamese claimed to have destroyed 320 American aircraft in air-to-air combat, though the US only acknowledged the loss of 92 and itself claimed 193 North Vietnamese aircraft in aerial combat.

In the spring of 1965 the USAF was opposed, first by MiG-17s and later by MiG-19s and 21s. Some of the USAF's first air-to-air combat losses occurred on 4 April 1965 when four North Vietnamese MiG-17s jumped a force of F-105 Thunderchief fighter bombers and F-100 Super Sabres, scoring two kills. Subsequently, on 17 June 1965 two F-4 Phantoms intercepted four MiG-17s, claiming two with radar-guided Sparrow missiles. Three days later four piston-engine A-1 Skyraiders took on two MiG-17s and shot one down with 20mm cannon fire. North Vietnam in mid-1966 had about sixty-five fighters, (most were MiG-17s, though they also included a dozen MiG-21s); by early 1972 this force had expanded to 200 (half of which were MiG-21s).

North Vietnam's anti-aircraft artillery (AAA) defences were formidable and accounted for up to 68 per cent of US aircraft losses. From 1967 to 1972 there were 200 SA-2 missile sites in North Vietnam, although by 1972 150 missiles were fired for every aircraft brought down, so they were not terribly effective. The USAF's experience with the SAM-2 and SAM-3 meant that the Americans were able to develop electronic countermeasures that were able to jam radar-guidance frequencies. This was to have a significant impact in later conflicts.

In support of operations America deployed assets such as the carrier-based RA-5C Vigilante, RF-101 Voodoo and RF-4C Phantom, the latter proving to be the most effective tactical reconnaissance aircraft of the war. In the spring of 1965 US intelligence officials received aerial photos of North Vietnamese SAM and AAA sites. The following year recon aircraft photographed MiG-17 interceptors at Phuc Yen airfield, north-east of Hanoi. Photography of MiG-21s showed that they were also appearing in increasing numbers. All this served to prove that Moscow was upping the ante in Vietnam.

Aerial imagery was used to assess and support the destruction of the Ho Chi Minh trail, the communist's main supply route, and enemy build-ups in the demilitarised zone. The South Vietnamese Army's attempts to cut the route in Laos in the early 1970s ended in disaster. Later US aerial reconnaissance photos confirmed the destruction by US air power of T-54 and PT-76 tanks, which had helped maul the South Vietnamese so badly. Such imagery also confirmed the first ever tank kill by a US helicopter at An Loc on 15 April 1972.

Crucially, American rules of engagement forbade bombing of the vital rail network or air bases in China's provinces bordering North Korea for fear of sparking a much wider war. Instead attacks had to be directed against the Ho Chi Minh and Sihanouk trails: these ran south through North Vietnam, Laos and Cambodia into South Vietnam and north through Cambodia and Laos into South Vietnam respectively. The Americans and South Vietnamese also had to contend with seaborne infiltrations. Weapon supplies were shifted down the Ho Chi Minh trail by truck and porters using bicycles. Despite the deployment of massive American air power and a sustained bombing campaign the trail was never completely cut.

Between January 1962 and August 1973 the USAF lost a staggering 2,257 aircraft to all causes at a cost of $3.1 billion. Personnel losses numbered 5,578 killed and wounded. Over 3,000 American and allied aircrew were rescued from the jungles. The Americans took pilot rescue very seriously: USAF's Aerospace Rescue Recovery Service lost forty-five aircraft on such operations.

American air power unleashed during the Tet Offensive was absolutely devastating. US naval air strikes were used in support of the marine defenders of Khe Sanh in early 1968; during February and March 3,100 sorties were flown by US carrier-based aircraft alone. US air support for Khe Sanh also included over 7,000 sorties by the 1st Marine Aircraft Wing. In total, over 24,000 tactical sorties and 2,500 B-52 bomber sorties were launched against the surrounding communist forces – an astonishing 100,000 tons of bombs was expended.

In particular the B-52s, dropping 75,000 tons of munitions over nine weeks, provided the heaviest firepower ever unloaded on a tactical target. General Giap himself almost became a victim of the B-52s when he visited Khe Sanh in late January 1968. In total, the B-52 was to make 126,663 sorties over South-east Asia. Operation Niagara even initially included consideration of tactical nuclear weapons.

The VNAF was to fly 7,213 sorties over four weeks, during which time it expended 6,700 tons of ammunition as well as transporting 12,200 men and 230 tons of supplies and equipment. During Tet the VNAF lost seventeen aircraft: ten on the ground and seven in the air, the latter comprising five A-1s, one C-47 and one U-17 (the high-wing Cessna 180 derivative). Overall, despite its relatively small size, the VNAF fought well.

The first American warplane to be supplied to the South Vietnamese Air Force was the Douglas AD-6 Skyraider. This prop-driven aircraft had been designed in 1944 and could take a large amount of punishment and still stay in the air. It was an ideal aircraft for the jungle war.

As North Vietnam's air defences grew stronger A-1E Skyraiders were restricted to missions over the South.

RADAR

BAMBOO MATTING

A close up of an SA-2 SAM site; four launchers have been highlighted and the radar is to the right.

The Cessna A-37B Dragonfly and the F-5E Tiger were used to bring the South Vietnamese Air Force up to strength and create an all-jet fleet. In August 1967 approximately ten Dragonflies arrived at Bien Hoa and Pleiku for evaluation by the USAF's 604th Fighter Squadron under project 'Combat Dragon'. The American A-37s were soon joined by Vietnamese-flown A-37s of the VNAF 524th Fighter Squadron at Nha Trang. The highly versatile A-37 was used for all light strike missions including counter-insurgency, forward air controller and rescue escort.

Pilots of the North Vietnamese Air Force. Initially the air force was only equipped with piston-powered trainers but in the early 1960s pilots began to undertake jet training in China and the USSR. This meant that, following the Tonkin incident, the NVAF was able to challenge the Americans with MiG-17 jet fighters.

The first F-4 Phantoms to fly in Vietnam, as opposed to operating from neighbouring Thailand, were those of the US Marine Corps, which arrived in April 1965. The two squadrons were known as the 'Grey Ghosts' and the 'Crusaders' and were painted in a gull grey with white undersides; however, by the end of the year the Phantoms were being camouflaged.

The North American F-100 Super Sabre was the heavy-duty bomb carrier over Vietnam and flew more sorties than any other aircraft type.

Due to the Tet Offensive and the heavy fighting at Hue, B-52 Stratofortress bombing sorties were increased from 800 to 1,200 a month. On 15 February 1968 this was increased to 1,800. The B-52F was the first model employed, but it was the B-52D with the 'Big Belly' modification, enabling them to carry up to 108 bombs, that became the main heavy bomber of the war. The B-52s operated from bases on Guam and in Thailand during the Vietnam War and the Operation Arc Light raids first hit Viet Cong jungle hideouts in mid-1965. The B-52 became one of the weapons that the VC and NVA most feared.

A typical North Vietnamese surface-to-air missile site with the SA-2 missile launchers surrounding their radars.

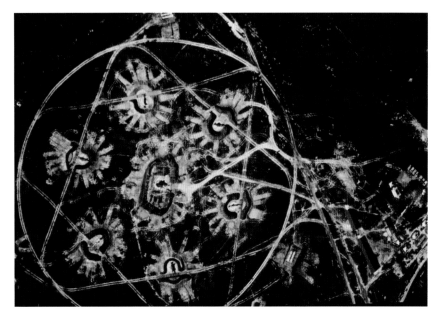

North Vietnamese pilots passing their MiG-17s. They downed an F-4 Phantom on 24 June 1967 and an F-105 the following day. The NVAF also flew MiG-21s in combat but the MiG-15s were only used for advanced training.

A briefing for North Vietnamese pilots. From 1965 onward the NVAF mainly operated the MiG-17F clear-weather interceptors, as well as some Chinese-built Shenyang F4s (the export version of the J-4). It also received some MiG-17PFs and MiG-17PFUs. During 1967–8 the NVAF suffered heavy losses and for all practical purposes effectively ceased to exist.

Fragments from this exploding SA-2 missile fatally damaged this USAF F-105D Thunderchief on 14 February 1968.

North Vietnamese pilots in Soviet anti-g suits prepare for a forthcoming mission. It was only the halt to American bombing missions on 1 November 1968 that enabled North Vietnam to rebuild its air force following Tet. They were to receive some MiG-19s, which were mainly the Chinese-built copy, the Shenyang F6 (the export version of the J-6).

This North Vietnamese MiG-17 was hit by 20mm rounds fired by an F-105D on 3 June 1967. Major Ralph L. Kuster's gun camera captured the moment that the MiG's external fuel tanks exploded, engulfing the entire left wing in flames. The MiG rolled over, just after Major Kuster passed below it, and crashed forty-one miles east-north-east of Hanoi. The kill was also shared with Captain Larry D. Wiggins; the men served with the 13th and 469th tactical fighter squadrons respectively.

American AQM-34 surveillance drones. The pointed-nosed R model was for high-altitude surveillance while the flat-nosed L model was the low-altitude photo workhorse.

Viet Cong with a wounded American POW.

The USAF's air-to-air refuelling capability gave its fighter bombers great range. The first shot shows 750lb-bomb-laden 'Thuds' or Republic F-105 Thunderchiefs lining up to take on fuel in December 1965. This aircraft bore the brunt of the air war against North Vietnam when Rolling Thunder commenced in 1965. They were based in Thailand where there was supposed to be an agreement preventing them operating over South Vietnam against the Viet Cong. The second shot shows F-4 Phantoms and F-105 Thunderchiefs refuelling from a Boeing KC-135 Stratotanker.

An NVAF MiG-21PF deploying its braking chute while landing after a mission.

The Martin RB-57E Canberra employed in the Patricia Lynn programme used a system called Compass Eagle to supply real-time, infra-red tracking of Viet Cong supply boats in the waters near Saigon. The aircraft would then call in artillery fire, gunships or patrol vessels to intercept the enemy supply vessels.

An American F-4 Phantom pilot is congratulated on his 200th mission. For ground-attack operations the Phantom usually carried bombs or napalm, but it could also launch rockets that were carried in pods under the wings.

American aircraft spraying defoliant agent onto the Vietnamese jungle. In 1968 the heavily forested War Zones C and D to the north-west and north of Saigon, which were Viet Cong strongholds, were regularly sprayed. While American aircrews were told Agent Orange was safe, the VC deliberately avoided crossing recently sprayed areas and would not camp in them.

USAF F-105D Thunderchiefs refuelling from Boeing KC-135A Stratotankers en route to North Vietnam.

Chapter Five

The Helicopter Comes of Age

Crucially, Giap had underestimated the technological strides that had been made since Dien Bien Phu. The helicopter and transport aircraft sustained the lifeline to Khe Sanh: indeed, air supply delivered 12,000 tons of cargo. In addition, over 600 parachute drops were made, which were vital for those men on the exposed hills. On the ground the communists did ensure that no support got through by keeping up their artillery attacks on American bases at Dong Ha, Con Thien and Camp Carroll.

The helicopter's first major conventional war was Korea, where such aircraft as the Sikorsky S-51/H-5 and Bell 47 were used for casualty evacuation and reconnaissance purposes. Four helicopters accompanied the 1st Provisional Marine Brigade to South Korea in 1950 and the first-ever helicopter evacuation of American casualties was performed by marine VMO-6 helicopters on 4 August 1950.

In the postwar period the helicopter was increasingly used in the colonial wars that beset the British and French empires. In Indochina the French first deployed American-built H-19B helicopters against the Viet Minh in 1954, though this was too late to help stave off defeat. France, determined not to lose Algeria as well, quickly became one of the world's leading authorities on the use of helicopters in combat conditions after buying further aircraft from the US. These included the Boeing Vertol OH-21 Work Horse/Shawnee. In order to protect these slow transports from the Algerian National Liberation Front, the French Army's 2nd Helicopter Group experimented with mounting machine guns on its aircraft for counter-insurgency operations.

Whilst the helicopter was used in assault operations in Korea, Suez and Algeria, the concept of massed helicopter air mobility was not fully appreciated until American intervention in South-east Asia. The Vietnam War was where the helicopter truly came into its own, playing a significant role in the bloody and protracted conflict. Not only did the helicopter prove its utility in a whole host of roles, the war also highlighted its extreme vulnerability to small-arms fire and ground fire in general. This was attested by the very high helicopter casualty rates.

In December 1961 former escort carrier USNS *Card* arrived off Saigon with thirty-two Vertol H-21 Shawnee helicopters. The following year the first Bell UH-1 Hueys were initially deployed for supply purposes, but quickly became pressed into service to ferry troops into action. By 1964 over 400 US Army aircraft had been deployed in theatre, including 250 UH-1 Hueys and nine CH-37 Mojave heavy transport helicopters. In total, about 5,000 Hueys were employed in Vietnam. The CH-46 Chinook medium-lift helicopter also earned its stripes in Vietnam.

The first US Army air mobile unit to be committed was the 173rd Airborne Brigade in June 1965, followed by the 1st Cavalry Division (Air Mobile) equipped with over 400 aircraft. The division, stationed at An Khe on Route 19, regularly had hundreds of helicopters airborne at any one time. By 1968 the South Vietnamese Air Force possessed about seventy-five H-34 helicopters; by the end of 1972 it had some 500 new machines, one of the largest, costliest and most modern helicopters fleets in the world at that time. Just three years later, with the South's collapse all were destroyed or had fallen into North Vietnamese hands.

The helicopter gunship, in particular the Bell AH-1G HueyCobra, which went operational in September 1967, also made its presence felt during this war. In the case of the Cobra it was the first time a rotary-wing aircraft was specifically designed for armed combat. Veterans of the Korea War, the Hiller UH-23 Raven and Bell OH-13 Sioux also saw service in Vietnam, though neither were as successful as the lighter Hughes OH-6A Cayuse. The Sikorsky CH-53A had the rather unique role in that its primary mission was to rescue crashed helicopters. During January–May 1967 they retrieved 103 aircraft, seventy-two of them CH-34s.

The first instance of a tank being destroyed by a guided-missile-firing helicopter did not occur until 2 May 1972, during North Vietnam's Easter offensive. Two UH-1Bs knocked out an NVA light tank using tube-launched, optically tracked, wire-guided (TOW) anti-tank missiles; in subsequent actions UH-1Bs went on to destroy another twenty-six tanks. On 13 April the following year the AH-1G Cobra got in on the act, using high-explosive, anti-tank (HEAT) missiles to knock out four NVA T-54 tanks near An Loc. There was little real novelty in this as helicopters and guided anti-tank missiles had been about since the Second World War. However, it had taken almost three decades to successfully mate the two technologies, and now the anti-tank helicopter is considered to be one of the most dangerous opponents of armoured fighting vehicles and fixed positions.

Whilst Vietnam established the helicopter's indispensability as a battlefield transport and aggressor, it also highlighted its vulnerability. Incredibly, over 16,000 were lost to enemy action or accident in Vietnam (though this equated to only one per every 400 sorties). Nonetheless, many were recovered and repaired, so that total combat losses amounted to 2,076, whilst accidents accounted for another

2,566. Only the Cobra proved to be particularly resilient: between September 1967 and June 1969 563 AH-1s were hit by ground fire, but only fifty-seven were actually destroyed.

The largest, longest-ranging combat helicopter assault was Operation Lam Son 719 on 6 March 1971, when 120 Hueys ferried two South Vietnamese infantry battalions 77km into Laos. They only lost one helicopter on the approach. This impressive success was marred by the shambles of the evacuation and by the fact that during Laotian operations between 8 February and 9 April 1971, the Americans lost 108 helicopters, with another 600 damaged – all of which helped hasten America's departure.

Ultimately the US forces and Army of the Republic of Vietnam's dependence on the helicopter was to prove a serious disadvantage – especially after the NVA became equipped with the Soviet man-portable SAM-7 anti-aircraft missile (effective against all subsonic aircraft below about 3,000m). It also ran contrary to the hearts and minds campaign by distancing the military from the indigenous population it was supposed to be protecting.

The Huey became the only way in and out of the base at Khe Sanh in 1968 in the face of the Vietnamese communist blockade. Over 5,000 American and ARVN helicopters were lost in Vietnam.

In September 1967 the first helicopter designed specifically as a gunship arrived in South Vietnam. This was the AH-1G HueyCobra: it had been ordered in 1966 as an escort helicopter to help reduce transport helicopter losses by providing effective fire suppression during air-mobile operations. It was armed with 40mm grenade launchers and a 7.62mm Minigun in the nose, with fifty-two 2.75in rockets in four pods beneath the stub wings. They offered a much thinner profile than the Bell UH-1s.

The US Army's aviation units began to get involved in December 1961 when the former escort carrier USNS *Card* arrived in Saigon with thirty-two Boeing Vertol H-21 Shawnee 'Banana' heavy troop carriers of the 8th and 57th transportation companies (light helicopter).

The workhorse of the Vietnam War: the UH-1 Huey first arrived in early 1962 and two years later there were 250 of them in Vietnam. For a while the conflict in South-east Asia was a helicopter war but as the conflict escalated it lost it pre-eminence.

The business end of a US 1st Cavalry Division (Air Mobile) Huey in Vietnam. The division incorporated elements of its predecessor, the 11th Air Assault Division, along with three other divisions in 1965.

This gives a clear view of the UH-1 Huey's pintle-mounted M60 machine gun. It also gives a strong impression of just how exposed the door gunners were. The UH-1D was first delivered in 1963, just in time for the Vietnam War, but in terms of combat units was superseded by the H model. As well as the door-mounted M60 machine gun, gunships were also armed with 40mm grenade launchers and 2.75in rockets.

A long-fuselage Huey – the short-fuselage models comprised the UH-1 A, B, C, E and P, while the longer bodies were designated the UH-1D, F, H and N.

A Huey spraying defoliant.

A side view of a US Army Huey.

A USAF Sikorsky HH-3E Jolly Green Giant helicopter of the 37th Aerospace Rescue and Recovery Squadron taking off from Da Nang air base in 1968. Such units were vital for rescuing downed pilots.

The epitome of the air-mobile Vietnam War, men of the US 2nd Battalion, 46th Infantry Regiment on a two-day search-and-destroy mission conducted against the Viet Cong in the Ben Luc area, April 1965.

A 1st Air Cavalry Huey dropping off troops during a combat assault. As a result of US involvement in South-east Asia, helicopter deployment and tactics reached their zenith. The 1st Air Cavalry alone could put 400 helicopters in the air over Vietnam.

The Bell UH-1 Huey was the workhorse of US forces in Vietnam and regularly picked up troops from 'hot' landing zones. This highly successful helicopter was used by more air forces and built in greater numbers than any other military aircraft since the Second World War.

A US Marine Corps Sikorsky S-58/H-34 Choctaw on patrol in 1965 over Vietnam. This helicopter first entered service a decade earlier and 166 saw action with French forces in Algeria.

A side view of an HH-53 helicopter of the 40th Aerospace Rescue and Recovery Squadron seen from the gunner's position on a helicopter of the 21st Special Operations Squadron.

A crew member fires a 7.62mm Minigun from the rear ramp of a USAF HH-53 rescue helicopter.

CH-47s and UH-1s picking up troops ready for a major air assault.

A member of the US 1st Cavalry Division photographed on the eve of the Tet Offensive on 27 January 1968 on Landing Zone Betty's water tower.

Development of the Boeing CH-47 Chinook commenced in 1956 to provide the US Army with an all-weather cargo helicopter. Over 550 had served in Vietnam by 1972, providing vital battlefield airlift capability or operating as armed 'go-go birds'. The later models mounted two 20mm Miniguns, a 40mm grenade launcher and a .50-calibre machine gun.

A US Navy CH-46 Sea Knight bringing in supplies. The CH-46 was the marine workhorse during much of the war, being employed for both combat assault in 'hot' areas and general heavy-lift duties.

Chapter Six

Here Comes the Armoured Cavalry

The NVA launched their attack at Lang Vei at 2230 hours on 6 February 1968 using elements of the 304th Division. Their plan was to occupy the base and ambush any relieving force. They quickly breached the wire and were in the forward trenches. From the observer tower on top of the camp's tactical operation centre (TOC) two PT-76 light tanks were spotted; five more were also seen approaching another position. Calls to Khe Sanh and Da Nang that enemy tanks were in the wire were met with initial disbelief. However, the defenders disabled three or four tanks and one was knocked out by an American aircraft (the first recorded tank kill by a helicopter did not occur until 1973 at An Loc), but the defenders were still overwhelmed at the perimeter and forced to flee the base.

The US Military Assistance Command Vietnam felt that armour had a minimal role to play in fighting the communists due to the terrain. General Westmoreland, commanding the US forces in Vietnam, even stated that 'except for a few coastal areas . . . Vietnam is no place for either tank or mechanized infantry units.' This meant that those US Army divisions that arrived in 1965 had no tanks or armoured personnel carriers.

In contrast, supporting the first US Marine Corps (USMC) landings at Da Nang on 8 March 1965 were the M48A3 Patton tank, along with the M50A1 Ontos anti-tank vehicle and LVPT-5A1 amphibian tractor (amtrac). These constituted the three main armoured fighting vehicles (AFVs) used by the marines during the Vietnam War. However, they also fielded the M67A2 flame-thrower and M51 Heavy Recovery Vehicle. The primary role of the USMC's tanks was in direct support of marine infantry operations with five tanks per infantry battalion. The Ontos, peculiar to the American marines, was a lightly armoured air-portable tracked vehicle, mounting six 106mm recoilless rifles. Designed as a tank killer it was mainly used for perimeter defence or bunker busting. The amtracs acted as troop and cargo carriers on land and at sea.

Once the VC guerrillas and NVA became more sophisticated, armoured-vehicle protection from small arms, rocket-propelled grenades and anti-personnel mines, plus increased mobility and firepower, became increasingly desirable. In 1966 the US 11th Armoured Cavalry Regiment and 25th Infantry Division arrived in South Vietnam complete with their armoured complement. These units achieved considerable success the following year.

The most important AFV of the war was undoubtedly the ubiquitous tracked M113. Most mechanised units in Vietnam employed it and it became known as the ACAV or armoured cavalry assault vehicle. Doctrine for mechanised infantry recognised that the APC's most important role was for transporting infantry safely to the battlefield, but the transport had a much wider role than this. Armoured cavalry also excelled as combat manoeuvre battalions rather than reconnaissance.

Whilst the Patton and M113 were the mainstay of American AFVs during the Vietnam War there were a host of others with specialised roles. These included the M551 Sheridan air mobile tank, M107 175mm and M109 155mm self-propelled artillery, M42A1 'Dusters' and M55 Quad 50s of the Air Defence Artillery battalions and the V-100 Commando armoured car. The 16th Armour of the 173rd Airborne Brigade was the only unit to use the Scorpion 90mm SPAT (self-propelled anti-tank gun). Ironically, the US, believing that missiles had superseded anti-aircraft artillery (AAA) had to retrieve its self-propelled guns from the Reserve and National Guard. As the North's air power was little threat, these weapons were used in a ground support role to devastating effect, firing 14 million 40/50mm rounds during the war.

In 1965 an Australian task force arrived with an APC troop. The Philippines also dispatched a security force consisting of seventeen APCs and two M41 tanks. The following year Royal Thai Army forces deployed an M113 platoon and a cavalry reconnaissance troop. South Korea also offered to supply a tank battalion, but the offer was turned down, though their forces were to deploy ACAVs in Vietnam.

A pivotal action took place in April 1966, showing the usefulness of US armour in jungle warfare. The US 1st Cavalry Division west of Plei Me requested self-propelled howitzer support. Nine M48A3s and seventeen M113s formed the escort for the guns like some old-fashioned wagon train. The column successfully ploughed its way through the jungle, and whilst the guns spent two days on firing missions the tanks searched the local hills for VC. The whole operation went off without mishap, convincing planners of the utility of armour.

Apart from American-built tanks the only others to be used in support of the South were the British-made Centurions of the 1st Australian Tank Force. In 1968 Australia sent twenty-six tanks and an additional cavalry platoon. Four squadrons served in Vietnam on a rotating basis from February 1968 to September 1971. They mainly operated in the Phuoc Tuy province east of Saigon near Vung Tau.

Although an NVA armoured force had been created as early as 1959, equipped with the Soviet-supplied T-54 and Chinese Type 59 main battle tanks, as well as

Soviet PT-76 light tanks, they did not make use of their armour until the closing years of the war. Up until 1972 NVA armour only appeared on or near the battlefields of South Vietnam on four recorded occasions.

Before the NVA's conventional invasion of the South, their only notable use of armour was at Lang Vei special forces camp near Khe Sanh on 6–7 February 1968 during the Tet Offensive, involving just thirteen PT-76 amphibious light tanks. PT-76 tanks of the 202nd Armoured Regiment also tried to overrun the special forces camp at Ben Het in March 1969. Two years later the NVA used them against ARVN troops in Laos and subsequently in their 1972 offensive.

By the early 1970s the US had begun to withdraw from South Vietnam and the NVA had become ever bolder in its use of tanks. The first major tank-versus-tank engagement took place in 1971 when the ARVN deployed armour during Operation Lam Son 719 (designed to cut the Ho Chi Minh trail in Laos) and found their M41A3 tanks up against NVA PT-76s and T-54s near Hill 31. For the loss of just four tanks they destroyed seven T-54s and sixteen PT-76s.

The ACAV crew spraying defoliant or insecticide round the perimeter of a base.

An M113 armoured personnel carrier in Vietnam – the folding armoured trim vane on the front is raised to stop water from washing over the hull when fording. Doctrine for mechanised infantry saw the armoured personnel carrier as simply a way of transporting infantry into battle. In Vietnam most units issued with the M113 used it as vehicle from which the troops fought. As a result the M113 was equipped with a variety of machine guns and armour shields. Known as the armoured cavalry assault vehicle (ACAV), it was the most important AFV of the war. This vehicle has a .50-calibre Browning machine gun as its primary armament with M60s mounted at the sides.

Combat experience soon demonstrated the need to protect the M113 crews. In 1966 a kit consisting of this 'bathtub' all-round protective shield for the commander's .50 Browning, plus shields for the two side-mounted M60 machine guns, created the ACAV.

ACAVs being used as assault vehicles in the jungles of Vietnam.

ACAVs guarding a river crossing in Vietnam.

M42A1 'Dusters' employed a light tank chassis to mount twin 40mm cannon and were especially useful in jungle fighting. The first shot shows a Duster in the MACV compound at Quang Tri City in February 1968.

The V-100, the Cadillac-Gage M706 Commando, was known as the 'Duck' from its shape or simply the 'V' from its designation. This was the principal armoured car employed in Vietnam by US forces and one of its primary roles was convoy escort. These particular vehicles are with the 31st Security Police Squadron at Tuy Hao air base in 1968.

Forward air controllers who could call in air strikes closely supported US and South Vietnamese ground forces. The Cessna O-1 Bird Dog saw extensive service with the US Army, US Marine Corps, USAF and the VNAF. Note the two rocket tubes slung under the wing – these were used for marking targets. With a top speed of 115mph, this aircraft was slow.

A mixed convoy of M48 Patton tanks and M113 armoured personnel carriers. The tank turrets have been built up to give the gunner some protection from small-arms fire when using the turret-mounted machine gun. In 1969, the peak year in terms of US involvement, there were 370 M48s serving in Vietnam.

An M67 flame tank in action; this was a variant of the M48, equipped with a flame-thrower. The vehicle commander is wearing the army-issue combat vehicle crewman's (CVC) helmet; both the US Army and US Marine Corps wore the CVC helmet. Flame tanks were often incorporated into the standard tank platoon.

US Marine Corps M48s. The first shot shows an AN-VSS-I searchlight mounted above the 90mm main armament on an M48A3, as the USMC transports 'grunts' of E Company, 2nd Battalion, 3rd Marines during 1966.

The M551 Sheridan, first deployed in 1969 with the ACAV troops, but it suffered from reliability problems and was particularly vulnerable to mines.

When the marines landed at Da Nang in 1965 the initial wave of assault troops came ashore in the LVTP-5A1 'amtrac'. Although intended for beach assaults they were redeployed as armoured personnel carriers as the marines began to sweep inland. These ones were photographed while on exercise on 19 April 1968.

A US 11th Armored Cavalry Regiment modified M113 ACAV in Vietnam. This unit pioneered the use of the ACAV, which came in a variety of variants, including the M106 mortar tracks, M548 tracked load carrier, M577 command vehicle and the M578 recovery vehicle.

VIÊT-CỘNG HÃY COI CHỪNG!!

VIET CONG BEWARE!

There is nowhere to run...nowhere to hide! The tanks and armored vehicles of the Blackhorse Regiment will find and destroy you! It is too late to fight. Beware Viet Cong, we are every-where! Rally now under the Chieu Hoi Program; it is your only hope to live!

A propaganda leaflet issued by the US 11th Armored Cavalry Regiment.

Chapter Seven

The Siege of
Khe Sanh and Lang Vei

Tet was intended to be the main communist offensive to conquer large parts of South Vietnam; General Giap believed that this, combined with an American defeat at Khe Sanh, would bring a swift end to the war. His grand strategy was to stretch the US/ARVN forces to a point where they would be unable to counter his primary goal. This it was hoped would spark a general rising of the South Vietnamese population, tired of its corrupt government, the war and the vast American military presence.

To MACV the siege of Khe Sanh in 1968 became the anvil upon which the communist Tet Offensive must falter. While initial intelligence reports indicated that Giap had committed everything to the Khe Sanh battle, General Westmoreland was rightly suspicious of the lull in the rest of South Vietnam and anticipated diversionary actions.

Planning for the relief of the marines at Khe Sanh began only four days after the battle started but soon had to be postponed because of the widespread nature of the other communist attacks. Indeed Khe Sanh was quickly forgotten on 30 January 1968 when the NVA launched their offensive with over 80,000 men. In fact some of the attacks were launched twenty-four hours prematurely, tipping off Westmoreland that something big was about to happen. General Phillip B. Davidson, MACV's intelligence chief, told Westmoreland that: 'This is going to happen in the rest of the country tonight and tomorrow morning.'

In the meantime, about 18,000 communist troops gathered for the main attack on Khe Sanh, including the 304th and 325C NVA divisions (which had gained fame thirteen years earlier at Dien Bien Phu – the symbolism of this was not to be lost on those involved) with twenty-seven light tanks plus heavy artillery that included eight 152mm, sixteen 130mm, thirty-six 122mm and twenty 100mm/105mm field guns, plus 120 rocket launchers. They were also equipped with fifty 37mm and 57mm anti-aircraft guns. Another division – the 320th near Camp Carroll, fifteen miles north-east – was positioned at Rock Pile, cutting Route 9. This obstructed

American military movements from Quang Tri and Dong Ha. The NVA's 324th Division was also available for the coming assault.

Helping to conceal communist movements, the weather changed, enveloping western Quang Tri province in thick fog. Under cover of this the NVA launched a bombardment on 24 January using 152mm artillery: the Americans suffered seven dead and seventy-seven wounded. The attackers also dug positions close enough to hit the indispensable airstrip with mortars. When the weather lifted on the 26th all American air operations across the whole of South Vietnam were concentrated in support of the besieged base, with 450 sorties that day. The ARVN's elite 37th Rangers Battalion was flown in and these men were to fight with distinction alongside the US marines. Forces also attempted to reopen Route 9, resulting in 150 VC and nineteen American dead.

Estimates of NVA strength reached 50,000 men: the 324B Division was deployed near Con Thien and Gio Linh, bringing communist forces up to 40,000 infantry plus 10,000 gunners, engineers and other support troops. Khe Sanh's garrison, consisting of the 9th and 26th US marine regiments, supporting artillery and the ARVN ranger battalion, were tying down over 20,000 NVA in the immediate vicinity. This was to have consequences for Giap's operations elsewhere.

Throughout Tet the communists did not let up their pressure on Khe Sanh, though the expected all-out assault to overrun the base never took place. Technology took a hand in its defence in the form of acoustic and seismic sensors (of which 250 were placed around the perimeter over a ten-day period). On 4 February it was reported that there were five NVA divisions south of the DMZ, now that the 308th Division had been bought into the area. This eavesdropping forewarned the marines that the communists were gathering near Hill 881 with a view to attacking it on 5 February.

However, the main assault was actually launched against Hill 861A, catching the defenders off guard and allowing the NVA/VC to almost overrun them. Recovering from the surprise Lieutenant Donald Shanley led his men in a counter-attack and for over thirty minutes a desperate hand-to-hand battle was fought. It was not until the barrage around Hill 881 had dispersed the diversionary attack and been brought to bear on 881A that the NVA/VC were finally driven off.

The NVA made little use of its armoured forces; except for the attack on Lang Vei special forces camp, when they deployed thirteen PT-76 light tanks. The garrison, under Captain Frank Willoughby, consisted of a special forces 'A' team of twenty-four Green Berets, four under-strength Civilian Irregular Defense Group companies of 400 Montagnards, a detachment of Vietnamese special forces and 500 Laotian soldiers (who had been driven over the border by NVA inside Laos). They were equipped with two 106mm and four 57mm recoilless rifles, two 4.2in and six 81mm mortars as well as M72 light anti-tank weapons (LAWs). The marine artillery at Khe Sanh to the east could be called on as well as AC-47 Spooky gunships in case of night attack, F-4 Phantoms and Huey helicopter gunships. Unfortunately a MACV directive dismissed the possibility of tank attack so the camp crucially had no anti-tank mines.

The NVA struck at 2230 hours on 6 February 1968 using elements of the 304th Division. Radio calls to Khe Sanh and Da Nang that enemy tanks were in the wire were met with surprise. Communication with Khe Sanh went as follows:

'Intrigue, Intrigue, this is Brass Study, over! We are taking a heavy ground attack and have armour in the wire. Stand by for fire mission over.'
'Brassy, this is Intrigue. Are you sure about the armour?'
'Roger, roger, that is affirm. We have tanks in the perimeter.'
'Can you see them from your location?'
'Affirmative, affirmative! I can hear the engines backfiring. They're firing into the bunkers!'
'Negative, Brassy. That must be the sound of your generators backfiring.'
'Intrigue, be advised one of our generators just blew down the bunker door!'

The commander at Khe Sanh was reluctant to send helicopters or ground forces to a 'hot site' at night. Route 9 was blocked and NVA tanks were on the landing zones. Instead artillery began to fire onto the perimeter and at 0100 hours F-4s and A-1 Skyraiders launched air strikes. A B-57 Canberra bomber triggered fifteen secondary blasts which may have damaged three or more of the NVA tanks. In the darkness and with nothing to counter effectively the remaining tanks organised resistance collapsed. The surviving defenders retreated to the tactical operation centre where they were trapped until 1600 the following day. Friendly fire was called down on the TOC and in the confusion Willoughby, thirteen Green Berets and sixty Montagnards escaped to be airlifted to Khe Sanh.

At the same time about 500 men of the 325C Division attacked thirty marines defending an outpost near Rock Quarry. The marines were driven from their positions and their officer killed. The following day, with massive fire support, it took the marines just fifteen minutes to recapture the outpost. As Lang Vei was falling the communists launched another attack at Khe Sanh, on 8 February, against the positions of the 9th Marines. The NVA/VC achieved half their objectives before massive air, artillery and tank support stopped them in their tracks. B-52s even dropped bombs to within 100 metres of the base's perimeter. Under cover of the air strikes and M48 Patton tanks a relief force drove off the attackers leaving 150 dead.

For five days the NVA/VC were pounded from the air. Then the weather closed in, enabling them to complete their elaborate siege network of tunnels, trenches and bunkers surrounding Khe Sanh. More importantly, anti-aircraft artillery on the surrounding hills proved effective against American cargo planes, forcing the Americans to rely on helicopters. Due to losses the US Seventh Air Force banned the C-130 Hercules from operating at Khe Sanh, leaving air supply to C-123 Providers. The loss of one of these and forty-eight lives on 6 March resulted in increasing reliance on helicopters. Khe Sanh was all but cut off.

US National Security Advisor Walt W. Rostow showing President Johnson a model of the Khe Sanh area in 1968.

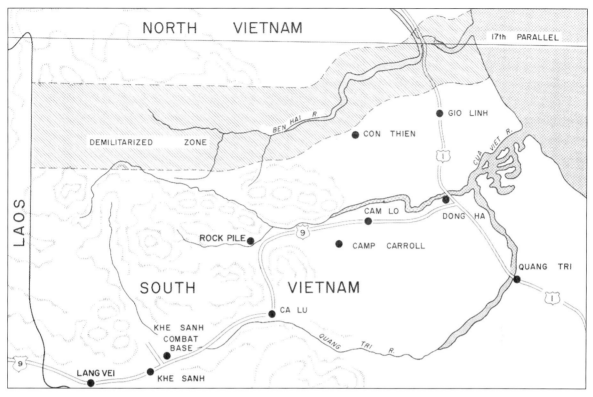

The northern Quang Tri province showing the location of Lang Vei, Khe Sanh and Camp Carroll. The camps' vicinity to the demilitarised zone and the Ho Chi Minh trail made them inevitable targets for the Tet Offensive.

During the siege of Khe Sanh communist forces did everything in their power to cut the US marines' vital air bridge. Engines revving, a C-130 transport aircraft at Khe Sanh has a narrow miss – despite enemy fire sweeping the runway. There were 273 landings by C-130 Hercules, 179 by C-123 Providers and eight by C-7 Caribous.

Members of the US 3rd Marine Division complete construction of M101 105mm howitzer positions at a mountain-top fire support base.

This shot gives some idea of just how exposed Khe Sanh's outlying defensive positions were. This CH-47 Chinook is bringing in much-needed supplies and taking out the wounded.

The garrison were supported by a number of Patton tanks.

A US Army M107 175mm self-propelled gun provides fire support from Camp Carroll to the east of Khe Sanh. During the battle marine gunners fired almost 159,000 rounds – in contrast, NVA gunners put just under 11,000 artillery and mortar rounds and rockets onto the marines' positions. The M107 could throw a 147lb (55kg) high-explosive shell out to a maximum range of 35,870 yards (32,785m).

NVA anti-aircraft artillery in the surrounding hills made it very hazardous for aircrews trying to resupply Khe Sanh.

A North Vietnamese rocket attack on Khe Sanh – heavy bombardment began on 21 January 1968 to divert US attention from the imminent nationwide offensive.

US marines work frantically to patch up Khe Sanh's runway after the latest mortar and rocket attack.

A C-7A Caribou comes in to land. Although a relatively small transport aircraft, it could carry around 6,000lb (2,721kg) of cargo or seventeen fully equipped soldiers, and could land in places often inaccessible to the C-123 or C-130.

Once the landing zone at Khe Sanh became too 'hot', air drop was about the only way to keep the garrison resupplied. In total some 496 parachute drops were made.

An F-100D Super Sabre lights up an enemy position. In the face of strong objections from the marines, who did not like subordinating their aircraft to the USAF's command, on 8 March 1968 General 'Spike' Momyer, the Seventh Air Force chief in Saigon, took charge of air operations in the Khe Sanh area. That year the regular air force F-100 units were supplemented by four air national guard squadrons.

A 'gun truck', comprising a 6x6 truck with an M55 Quadmount .50-calibre gun, at Khe Sanh during the battle. Such field modifications were designed to provide convoy protection for the transport companies. Originally intended as an anti-aircraft weapon the Quadmount .50 proved to be an effective perimeter weapon at fire support bases.

The C-130 Hercules had been designed for the low-altitude parachute extraction system (LAPES) that enables the aircraft to off-load without touching the ground. However, the casualties at Khe Sanh still had to be picked up by the C-130s and C-123s.

American troops examining a knocked-out NVA PT-76 amphibious light tank. The attack on the Lang Vei special forces camp involved thirteen of these vehicles.

The 1968 B-52 bombings in support of Khe Sanh became the largest such campaign so far. While anti-war protestors in America saw the deployment of the B-52 in South-east Asia as wasteful and ineffective, the marines at Khe Sanh witnessed the siege being broken up by heavy bombing. Operating above the clouds the bombs often came as a surprise and had devastating physical and psychological effects on VC troop concentrations.

An NVA crew with their Soviet-supplied SA-2 launcher. North Vietnamese surface-to-air missiles only accounted for 5 per cent of US combat losses; this was because of the effectiveness of American electronic countermeasures and the Wild Weasel air defence suppression missions.

The Strela-2, better known by its NATO reporting name SA-7 Grail, according to some sources entered service with the NVA in 1968 and was used to defend the Ho Chi Minh trail. Officially, though, it did not make its presence felt until 1972.

A US Navy Lockheed OP-2E Neptune – these were employed during the 'Igloo White' programme to drop sensors along the Ho Ch Minh trail from 1967. Using this intelligence AC-47s, A-26s and AC-123Bs acted as truck busters. This programme singularly failed to prevent the communist build-up for the Tet Offensive.

Chapter Eight

Battle of Hue

Outwardly MACV put a brave face on the situation in early February 1968, but behind the scenes General Westmoreland and his command were in a state of near panic. He clung to the belief that Khe Sanh was the enemy's key objective, despite the fact that much of South Vietnam was now under general attack, stretching all the way from Khe Sanh in the north to Ca Mau in the far south. He had expected that the enemy's effort would be directed against South Vietnam's northern provinces and his men were deployed accordingly. Westmoreland saw the military situation the opposite way to Giap, thinking that the attack on the cities was an effort to divert attention away from Khe Sanh.

Within just five days of the Tet Offensive commencing thirty of South Vietnam's forty-four provincial capitals, including Hue, had fallen to the communists. Despite the widespread attacks two areas emerged as major targets – the cities of Saigon and Hue. These were the only places where the fighting was particularly protracted. The communists' real success was at Hue where the NVA's 4th and 6th regiments and six VC battalions under General Tran Do captured most of the city and held it for a month.

Hue was located in the north of South Vietnam on the banks of the Huong, or Perfume, River, just a few miles inland from the South China Sea. The river gained its name as a result of the huge number of flowers from orchards that fall into the water every autumn, giving it a perfume-like aroma. Hue was once a fortified imperial capital and between 1802 and 1945 was the seat of power for the Nguyen dynasty.

Due to its strategic location, in 1968 Hue should have been well garrisoned. Considering its proximity to the DMZ (only 50km), Highway One passing through Hue was a vital supply route for ARVN, US and allied forces heading north from the coastal city of Da Nang to the DMZ; the highway gave access to the Perfume River in Hue itself, dividing the city into northern and southern areas. Hue was also a base for US Navy supply boats.

Communists objectives at Hue were the Tay Loc airfield, the ARVN's 1st Division headquarters in the citadel at Mang Ca, and the MACV compound in the New City on the south side of the river. The grounds of the citadel were surrounded by a wall and bordered by a moat fed by the Huong. Inside the citadel was the Imperial City, with a perimeter of almost 2.5km. Inside this was the imperial enclosure called the Purple Forbidden City.

As with all the communist assaults across South Vietnam, the seizure of Hue was a race against time before the ARVN and its US allies could muster enough forces for localised counter-attacks. While General Tran Do mustered around 10,000 men for the attack, General Truong, the commander of the weak ARVN 1st Division garrison, was able to call on forces from outside the city. These included ARVN infantry, armoured and airborne units, while to the south-east of Hue there were three US Marine Corps battalions protecting the Phu Bai air base, Highway One and all the western approaches to the city. To keep the marines occupied the communist forces had to attack the air base and the Truoi River and Phu Loc areas.

Phu Bai was also home to marine helicopters, including the White Knights medium helicopter squadron of HMM-165 as well as transport aircraft. It was a sprawling base consisting of a series of compounds housing barracks, workshops, hangers and stores either side of the runway. This air base supported all the isolated hilltop outposts in the region, many of which were reliant on helicopters for resupply. Throughout the last two-thirds of January 1968 HMM-165 was very busy, flying 2,508 sorties that moved 3,851 troops and over 400 tons of supplies.

Base defences included 6in and 8in howitzers, towed and self-propelled respectively, which meant this was not a facility that could be easily assaulted by the NVA/VC. An all-out attack was not feasible in light of the resources being committed to the main attack on Hue. Instead they subjected the base to rocket attack, which caused some damage – hitting at least one hanger, peppering a CH-46 helicopter in shrapnel and cratering the street in front of some of the barrack buildings. The marines quickly moved to drive the attackers away from the perimeter in order to safeguard the flightlines and runway.

Key amongst the ARVN reinforcements were the 1st Airborne Task Force located 17km north of Hue and two battalions of the 3rd Regiment with the 7th Armored Cavalry Squadron (which was equipped with M24 Chaffee light tanks) based to the south-west. Again NVA/VC blocking forces would have to fight to prevent these units getting into the city.

The assault on Hue started in the early hours of 31 January 1968; the NVA 6th Regiment attacked the western bank of the citadel with the aim of seizing the Mang Ca compound, the Tay Loc airfield and the imperial palace. The NVA 4th Regiment assaulted the MACV compound in the southern part of the city. The western gate was seized and the NVA 800th and 802nd battalions drove north. At Tay Loc the 800th was stopped by the ARVN Hac Bao or 'Black Panthers' Strike Company and the 802nd was thwarted at Mang Ca by an ad hoc force of 200 South Vietnamese troops.

South of the city the ARVN's 7th Armoured Cavalry Squadron attempted to fight their way into Hue. Although they got over the An Cuu bridge into the New City, the column was forced to retreat after its commander, Lieutenant Phan Hu Chi, was killed. To the south-east the US marines at Phu Bai air base also found themselves under attack, but 1st Battalion, 1st Marines was despatched to Hue with its tanks and fought its way to the MACV compound. Marine M48 and ARVN M24 tanks were then sent to secure the bridge over the Perfume River. They soon found that the area of Hue north of the river had fallen to the enemy, who had dug in.

The attack on Hue was launched on the same day as the attack on Saigon and by nightfall the NVA/VC had raised their flag over the ancient citadel. During the day US/ARVN forces pushed into the city to rescue some American advisers and then promptly withdrew. Only in Hue did the attackers receive any measure of local support – principally from the pro-communist student population. The commitment of US/ARVN troops to the defence of Khe Sanh and other locations in the northern provinces had the desired effect, for there was a critical delay in gathering sufficient reinforcements to regain control of Hue.

The marines were ready by early February after Lieutenant-General Cushman, I Corps Marine commander, and Lieutenant-General Lam, Vietnamese force commander, had rounded up enough men. Three US marine and eleven ARVN battalions had to fight a bloody three-week battle for Hue. The communist forces refused to withdraw or surrender. They hoped that the longer they held out the more likely they were to spark a general rising.

One problem that arose, which was not an issue in Saigon, was that Hue was full of sacred religious and historical buildings. Initially the attackers showed restraint in using artillery and air power but it rapidly became apparent that the only way to force the enemy out of the city would be to destroy it building by building. When the marines approached the citadel the NVA/VC defenders blew up the main bridge over the Perfume River. For four days the marines were held on the far banks in the full knowledge that they would have to storm the ancient fortifications and clear it inch by inch. Eventually they forced a crossing and surrounded the citadel.

From 11 to 15 February the South Vietnamese forces, with American support, fought to clear the rest of the city. The street fighting was bitter; even after intensive bombardment the surviving NVA/VC converted the rubble into strongpoints. The assault on the citadel did not commence until 20 February, but within two days the communist forces only held the south-western corner and on the following day even that position was finally eliminated. On 25 February the whole city was described as secure.

Wholesale death and destruction had been wrought on the once beautiful city. Its streets and ancient temples lay in ruins. The communists lost 8,000 men in Hue and the surrounding area. Allied forces lost 668 dead and 3,707 wounded. There were also some 5,000 civilians killed, many of whom were executed by the communists. Over 100,000 Vietnamese were made homeless by the battle of Hue. The losses on both sides were so heavy that each claimed it as a victory.

This Viet Cong could be a main force soldier or an irregular. His headgear is a Chinese-manufactured plastic sun helmet covered with waterproof nylon. The man's weapon is a Chicom Type 56 carbine, the Chinese copy of the Soviet SKS.

Communist objectives at Hue included the Tay Loc airfield which was inside the citadel – also known as the Hue Citadel airfield – the runway was 2,400 feet long. This was the base of the Hac Boa or Black Panther Ranger Company, the bodyguard of the ARVN 1st Division commander. The American presence included MACV Advisory Team 3 and members of the US 20th Tactical Air Support Squdron who were flying forward-air-controller missions.

Exhausted-looking US marines – for the Americans the fighting in Hue was perhaps the most intense of the entire war. These men are from H Company, 2nd Battalion, 5th Marine Regiment. Brigadier General Foster Lahue, a veteran of the Second World War and Korean War, who commanded the marines at Hue called the fighting 'among the worst in our history'.

These gunners are laying down fire with the 23lb M60 that served as the rifle squad's standard automatic weapon. This machine gun could spit forth 100 rounds of 7.62mm ammunition per minute. The weight of the weapon and its tremendous rate of fire mean that M60 gunners normally had to have an assistant to carry extra ammunition and help in the gun's operation. An additional 100 rounds of the belted ammunition came in cardboard boxes.

A marine rushes past an M48 Patton during the street fighting in Hue. Judging by his bare arms he has chosen to forego wearing OGs or a T-shirt under his flak vest. The large square box at the base of the 90mm gun is a xenon searchlight, this was used to blind an opponent and light up the battlefield.

An ARVN command post calling in either artillery or air strikes on communist positions.

The Vought A-7 Corsair, intended as a successor to the A-4 Skyhawk light attack aircraft, was first deployed to the Gulf of Tonkin in December 1967.

The ARVN calling in air strikes in the A Shau Valley.

F-4 Phantoms – attempts to safeguard Hue's ancient buildings from air attack were quickly abandoned. These two USAF McDonnell F-4D-30-MC Phantom II fighters are from the 435th Tactical Fighter Squadron, 8th Tactical Fighter Wing, and were photographed over Vietnam from a Boeing KC-135A Stratotanker. Both Phantoms are armed with three SUU-30/B cluster bombs (right wing), three LAU-3 rocket launchers (left wing) and six Mk 82 227kg bombs (centreline).

The Vought F-8 Crusader. In early February 1968 when the 1st and 5th marines attempted to enter Hue the weather improved slightly, allowing the F-8E Crusaders and A-4 Skyhawks to support the men on the ground. While the Navy variants were seldom seen with wing pylons the USMC aircraft were rarely seen without them. Marine Crusaders were operated from Da Nang during 1965–7 and were then withdrawn and reissued to the smaller US Navy carriers that could not take the Phantom 11.

A Douglas EB-66E Destroyer. These ECM platforms were vital in helping to keep losses to NVA SAMs to a minimum. Flying from bases in Thailand the B-66 force was kept busy until the advent of effective ECM carriage by the strikers themselves.

USAF and VNAF air strikes quickly began to target NVA/VC troop concentrations once the weather cleared in the Hue area. In the battle for the city 290,877lbs of aerial ordnance were delivered, along with 18,091 artillery rounds and 5,191 naval rounds.

The M18A1 anti-personnel Claymore mine. Electronically detonated it would shoot 700 tiny steel balls out to a range of fifty-four yards. The lightweight Claymore was used for defending positions and springing ambushes on enemy forces.

US marines disembarking from a C-123.

US troops escorting South Vietnamese civilians to safety. Great swathes of Hue were destroyed in the fighting, leaving 100,000 people homeless.

US forces in the shattered remains of a forest – once Hue was pacified the surrounding countryside had to be cleared of enemy forces.

An Operation Ranch Hand UC-123 spraying defoliant on a roadside in central South Vietnam. Ranch Hand crews flew over 19,000 sorties from 1962 to 1968. The year before the Tet Offensive almost 1,500,000 acres of forest and 200,000 acres of crops were sprayed.

The Hue forward air controllers at Tay Loc were in the process of transitioning to the new Cessna O-2A Skymaster and four were delivered on 30 January 1968 just prior to the attack. These were destroyed on the ground along with four O-1s that they were replacing. The Skymaster was used in a forward-air-controller role and could carry two Minigun pods for suppressive fire while white phosphorus rocket pods were used for marking targets. Its speed of up to 200mph and its agility meant that it was much less vulnerable than the O-1 Bird Dog; its only drawback was that it was larger and noisier.

Chapter Nine

Battle of Saigon

While the fighting in Hue to suppress the communist forces resulted in a bloodbath so did the fighting in South Vietnam's capital city. The battle for Saigon quickly turned into a public relations disaster for Washington as it struck at the very heart of America's military commitment to South Vietnam. The one place that the public assumed to be safe was swiftly shown to be a house of cards. In the months preceding the Tet Offensive NVA/VC personnel quietly and efficiently infiltrated the city to gather intelligence, finalise their plans and to establish secret weapons depots.

Although Saigon was the main focal point for the Tet Offensive, the complete seizure of the capital by the VC and NVA was simply not possible. Instead the communist forces selected six key targets, which thirty-five battalions of Viet Cong were to attack and hold. The sites chosen were predictably the military administrative hubs of Saigon: namely the ARVN's HQ, the Independence Palace, the US embassy, the sprawling Tan Son Nhut air base, the Long Binh naval HQ, and the national radio station.

In addition the VC 5th Division was to launch diversionary attacks on the military bases at Long Binh and Bien Hoa. The NVA 7th Division was tasked with striking the US 1st Infantry Division and the ARVN 5th Division at Lai Khe was to keep them tied down. Likewise the VC 9th Division was to assault the US 25th Infantry Division base at Cu Chi.

The major prize in Saigon was undoubtedly the massive air base at Tan Son Nhut. It was first developed in the early 1930s when the French colonial government constructed a small airfield with unpaved runways near the village of Tan Son Nhut. By mid-1956, with US aid, a 7,200-foot runway had been built and the airfield became South Vietnam's principal international gateway. By 1968 it was one of the busiest military air bases in the world. If the communist forces could overrun this it would be a cause of great embarrassment and humiliation to MACV. In addition, destruction of the aircraft and helicopters on the flightline would prevent them conducting ground-attack operations. This would be vital in holding up inevitable counter-attacks.

Likewise, as the US military presence in South Vietnam expanded, MACV rapidly outgrew its HQ at 137 Pasteur Street in central Saigon. In the summer of 1966 work started on a new HQ near Tan Son Nhut and the ARVN Joint General Staff compound came into being. Due to its size this new headquarters became grandly known as Pentagon East. MACV, though, was an administrative hub largely staffed by liaison officers, clerks and intelligence personnel.

Tan Son Nhut was not only the location of USAF's Seventh Air Force HQ, the South Vietnamese Air Force's HQ and the Joint General Staff of South Vietnam HQ, but also the VNAF's primary command facility. Most of the VNAF's operational units were deployed from the nearby Bien Hoa air base. Nonetheless, Tan Son Nhut still handled a huge volume of air traffic – particularly transport aircraft, helicopters and reconnaissance flights – as the central hub for South Vietnam. Due to the Tet holiday most of the VNAF personnel were on leave, but once the attack started a recall was issued and within seventy-two hours 90 per cent of the VNAF had returned to the base.

The US embassy in Saigon was first established in May 1950, and had also recently moved into a new building on a more secure compound in September 1967. Following the bomb attack two years earlier, it was decided that a new $2.6 million embassy with greater protection would be constructed. The site selected was a three-acre site known as the Norodom compound at No 4 Thong Nhut (now Le Duan) Boulevard at the corner of Thong Nhut and Mac Dinh Chi Street. This was in the heart of the diplomatic quarter and was next door to the French embassy, opposite the British embassy and located near to the presidential palace.

The new embassy comprised two separate compounds: the consular one sealed off by a separate wall and steel gate and the embassy compound with the embassy chancery building; behind it was a parking lot, a two-storey villa used as a residence by the mission coordinator (a civilian assistant to the US ambassador), a motor pool and other facilities. There were two entry gates, a pedestrian entrance on Thong Nhut Boulevard and a vehicle entrance on Mac Dinh Chi Street.

The new US chancery was a distinctive six-storey, white concrete building, with a concrete lattice facade that served to both cool the building and deflect rockets and other projectiles. A small helipad was located on the roof. A concrete awning extended from the chancery out over the pedestrian entrance on Thong Nhut Boulevard. It was one of the tallest buildings in Saigon at the time of its construction and was hard to miss. Crucially, neither the Tan Son Nhut/MACV facilities nor the US embassy were particularly well guarded. NVA/VC intelligence gauged that they were achievable goals.

By a stroke of luck Colonel Farley Peebles, commander of the 377th Combat Support Group responsible for security at Tan Son Nhut, had been forewarned. The Joint Defense Operation Center received intelligence thirty days prior to the attack indicating that something would happen over the Tet holiday. The intelligence suggested rocket or mortar attacks plus a ground assault of up to battalion strength. As a result, on 27 January a security exercise was conducted, focusing on Gate 051 as this was considered the most vulnerable point in the perimeter. Following this, USAF's 377th Security Police Squadron and the US Army's Task Force 35 remained on a heightened state of alert. While the security police and Task Force 35 were well trained and disciplined, they were neither equipped nor prepared to counter a regiment-sized enemy assault.

At 0300 hours on 31 January 1968 some 5,000 NVA/VC troops under General Tran Van Tra successfully infiltrated Saigon and launched their surprise attack. Over 700 men attacked Tan Son Nhut outside the city and the neighbouring MACV compound in order to eliminate the command post of the US Seventh Air Force. Because it was Tet (the Vietnamese New Year), the sound of firecrackers exploding masked any gunfire, giving the communists an element of surprise. In fact the surprise was so complete that the entire force slipped into Tan Son Nhut without the alarm being raised. The NVA/VC forces got to within 1,000 yards of their objective before being challenged. It was then that the shooting started.

Enemy rockets or mortar bombs first hit Tan Son Nhut at 0200 on 31 January with the base chapel taking a direct hit. Then at 0330 the guards at one of the northern bunkers gave the alarm that several hundred men were moving in from the west. Also the inhabitants of Bunker 051 reported that grenades and mortar rounds were being fired towards the western perimeter but were falling short. Colonel Peebles was alerted and his meagre security force suddenly found itself in the thick of it. If it had not been for the determined action of the 377th Security Squadron, Task Force 35 and the US 3rd Squadron, 4th Cavalry Regiment the communists would have penetrated the base even further than they did.

The major NVA/VC ground penetration was carried out along a line from Bunker 049 to Gate 051 on the western perimeter. Penetration attempts were also conducted at Gate 10 on the south-east perimeter and the MACV annex adjacent to Gate 10. At the point of penetration some men of the ARVN 2nd Services Battalion deserted their posts – whether this was in panic or deliberate was not known. At 0415 the 2nd Services Battalion commander committed a platoon of his reaction force with two US advisers to the Gate 051 area. They got to within 100 metres of Bunker 051 before being met by heavy fire from the enemy occupying the bunker. Shortly after, two ARVN light tanks were knocked out near Gate 051 and a third was forced to withdraw. At 0630 a counter-attack was launched, led by two companies from the ARVN's 8th Airborne Battalion.

An NVA unit dressed in ARVN uniforms infiltrated the South Vietnamese Joint General Staff HQ and turned the machine guns that were mounted to guard the installation on the surprised inhabitants. South Vietnamese officers had to barricade themselves in and fight a desperate defensive action until help could reach them. The heavy fighting around the MACV compound forced General Westmoreland to withdraw to his command bunker and order his staff to draw weapons to assist the defenders in beating off the attackers. The US compounds were garrisoned almost entirely by support troops, maintenance personnel and aircrew – who were all not accustomed to firing their weapons in anger.

Bunker 051 was finally recaptured by the US security police at 1210; by this stage it was the last area inside the base perimeter held by the enemy. In the process four of the USAF policemen were killed – they, along with two other combat security policemen, received the Silver Heart for bravery. ARVN airborne and marine units were then committed to clear the depot area of Hong Tong Tay that was under siege by VC forces. The intensity of the fighting on the base was such that the security detachments, with support from other units, killed almost 1,000 NVA/VC soldiers. The US Army also lost nineteen killed, the VNAF five and the ARVN twenty-seven.

The planned attacks were also staged against the palace, the radio station, US Navy HQ, the Philippine embassy and the US embassy. The city erupted to the sound of widespread gunfire and explosions. At the US embassy nineteen NVA/VC commandos disguised as civilians nearly overwhelmed the marine guards. Only five marines were on duty that night, just one more than usual. The fighting at the embassy lasted five hours and was later dubbed the 'battle for Bunker's bunker' as the ambassador was Ellsworth Bunker. The marines were eventually relieved by two platoons of the US 101st Airborne Division.

An NVA/VC suicide squad attacked the Independence Palace, while other units attacked the national police barracks, the radio station, army billets and anything remotely linked to the US and South Vietnamese governments. The Chinese suburb of Cholon was occupied by the communist forces and an HQ set up in An Quang Pagoda. The communists quickly set about rounding up anyone linked to the South Vietnamese government and the US military. In the districts they conducted summary trials along with summary executions. Martial law was declared in Saigon and a curfew imposed.

For a while chaos reigned across the city as enemy guerrilla units popped up everywhere. It took until 5 February to stabilise the situation and confine enemy resistance to the suburb of Cholon. It soon became apparent that this area had been the original staging post for the assault on Saigon. While the ground troops struggled to regain control, USAF B-52 bombers attacked suspected enemy troop concentrations ten miles from the capital. This was the closest the big bombers came to the city and, although they hit their targets, subsequent intelligence confirmed only forty-two kills, none of whom could be positively identified as communist troops.

According to US intelligence an estimated nine enemy battalions were committed to the greater Saigon area, and at least seven of them were involved in the attack on Tan Son Nhut air base. Those battalions in the Saigon area were supported by about twelve companies from the NVA's 5th Division. The VC 267th Battalion, a quarter of which were NVA troops, was the lead battalion in the assault on the western perimeter of Tan Son Nhut. Small-arms fire and probing actions against various parts of the base's perimeter continued through to 9 February. After all the VNAF personnel had been rounded up over the next three weeks its pilots then flew over 1,300 sorties, attacking communist troop concentrations throughout South Vietnam. Reconnaissance aircraft also conducted almost 700 sorties flying their O-1 Bird Dog and U-17 Skywagon aircraft gathering intelligence and calling in air strikes.

The Americans and the ARVN, supported by tanks, artillery, helicopters and ground-attack aircraft, fought to drive 1,600 communists from their stronghold in Cholon. However, NVA/VC forces launched a counter-attack from Cholon and other parts of the city on 18 February. Tan Son Nhut was attacked once more but the NVA/VC got no further than the outer perimeter as the defenders were fully on their guard this time. Reports estimated that up to three NVA divisions were outside the city, but they failed to get in and Cholon was pacified three days later. Although skirmishing continued on the outskirts of the city, the Tet Offensive in Saigon was over.

Saigon was accustomed to terrorist attacks but the scale of the Tet Offensive came as a complete shock. NVA/VC forces infiltrated the city with ease and were poised when General Tran Van Tra gave the order to attack on 31 Janaury 1968.

USAF security police defending the perimeter of Tan Son Nhut air base in response to a Viet Cong attack on 31 Jan 1968. The 377th Security Police Squadron had just conducted a security exercise and was on a heightened state of alert. Up until 1965 the ARVN was responsible for USAF installation security but, following the creation of USAF Security Police, a three-zone defensive system was developed, though in 1968 this was found to be too static.

An F-4 Phantom with an ordnance load consisting of air-to-air missiles. USAF and VNAF air power eventually helped turn the tide against the Tet Offensive. More F-4 fighters and RF-4 reconnaissance aircraft were lost in South-east Asia than any other aircraft type.

Progressively replaced by the A-4, A-6 and A-7, the single-seat A-1 Skyraider was last deployed by VA-25 Attack Squadron. From April 1965 through to April 1968 the squadron made three deployments in support of the Vietnam War, still flying the A-1. In January 1968 squadron aircraft provided close air support for US marines besieged at Khe Sanh. On 14 February a VA-25 A-1H was shot down by a MiG while operating from the USS *Coral Sea*.

Rows of exposed VNAF aircraft at Tan Son Nhut.

Most USAF Phantoms were stationed in Thailand and flew missions over North Vietnam. The Phantom also became a familiar sight in South Vietnam and often came to the aid of US or ARVN troops.

The McDonnell RF-4C Phantom began operations from Tan Son Nhut airfield in October 1965. They conducted nearly all the tactical reconnaissance in South Vietnam from 1968 onwards, so in part were responsible for missing the Tet Offensive build-up.

Once the communist attack got underway Tan Son Nhut airfield became the focus of a series of attacks conducted against Saigon. This F-4 was a victim of the heavy fighting in and around the airbase.

US troops repelling a VC attack.

A forward air controller flies a Cessna O-1E Bird Dog at low altitude to locate ground targets, guide in air strikes and coordinate air and ground fire.

A USAF forward air controller's twin-turbo-prop OV-10A Bronco fires rockets to mark an enemy position for a nearby F-100 Super Sabre. The latter was used for in-country operations in South Vietnam; its role peaked in 1968 when four air national guard squadrons supplemented USAF units. One of the new aircraft types that joined the fighting over South Vietnam in 1968 was the Bronco which deployed to Bien Hoa in late July, thereby missing Tet. It was flown by US Air Force, Navy and Marine units and, though primarily a FAC aircraft, the navy also used it in a light attack role.

Grumman A-6 Intruders unload their Mk 82 bombs – the Intruder could carry 15,000lb of bombs. This type of aircraft was capable of all-weather operations and began combat missions in July 1965 with VA-75 flying from the USS *Independence*. Its accuracy, enabling all-weather strikes, resulted in it being dubbed the 'mini-B-52'.

Civilians pick through the debris in Cholon. ARV rangers and the US 9th Infantry Division fought to retake the suburb while the US 7th Infantry Regiment secured the Phu Thu race track near Cholon. The US 47th Infantry Regiment engaged NVA positions south of 'Y' Bridge. From 5 to 12 May 1968 Saigon had to endure a 'mini-Tet', during which communist forces lost another 3,000 killed. Yet another attack was launched on 25 May.

Sweep operations always involved 'tunnel rats' who would have to clear out VC hideouts. These men are from the US 1st Cavalry Division (Air Mobile) and were photographed during Operation Oregon in Quan Ngai province in April 1967. A year later they found themselves flying to the relief of Khe Sanh following the assault of the Tet Offensive.

NVA/VC troops killed during the attacks on Tan Son Nhut. During the attacks at Bien Hoa and Tan Son Nhut over 2,000 VC were killed before the bases were secured. The best Viet Cong units had led the Tet assault and they were decimated: 38,794 were killed and 6,991 captured.

Chapter Ten

Air Mobile to the Rescue

Throughout South Vietnam many other cities were attacked, though not with the same ferocity as Saigon and Hue. In the Mekong Delta south of Saigon the cities of My Tho, Ben Tre, Vinh Long and Can Though saw guerrilla action. North of the capital, Bien Hoa, Dalat, Nha Trang, Qui Nhon, Quang Ngai up to Da Nang suffered in the fighting. By mid-March all of those lost cities had been returned to full South Vietnamese control. Nonetheless the devastation and chaos was such that it was hard to imagine anyone claiming victory.

Although the South Vietnamese and US counter-attacks across the country drove the enemy back, thirteen of the forty-four provinces of South Vietnam were thrown into such chaos that the gains made by the previous pacification programme were completely lost. Although the South Vietnamese government managed to regain control of the cities, hundreds of thousands of Vietnamese were homeless and thousands killed and wounded. At least 750,000 people needed rehoming.

Although Tet was largely over by 26 February 1968, Khe Sanh remained under siege and just three days later a large-scale night attack was launched against the base. The sensor technology again warned the defenders of the build-up at the eastern end of the main perimeter. Artillery, tactical aircraft and B-52 bombers ensured the attack died out before it reached the ARVN rangers' positions. During March the 325C Division to the north and the 304th Division to the south squeezed the base. Elements of the two divisions launched another attack on 17 March with the view to destroying the perimeter defences. The following day an NVA battalion tried to exploit the weakened sector and persisted for two hours before the marines repulsed them with heavy casualties.

Probing attacks continued, then – perhaps signalling a weakening of communist resolve – they switched to artillery bombardment. At the end of March the besieging forces had fallen to about 10,000. The 325C Division's HQ had withdrawn to Laos. Between 23 and 24 March the artillery fire was such that the marines were confined to their bunkers. In two days the base endured some 1,265 incoming rounds. The defenders, though, remained active, launching a raid against an NVA battalion position less than a kilometre from the base, killing 115. A total of 1,602 NVA bodies were found in the immediate area of Khe Sanh, though overall enemy losses were estimated at 10,000–15,000.

By now time for the attackers was running out, Tet was at an end and the situation in South Vietnam stabilised. The Americans and the ARVN put together a relief force, numbering 30,000 troops, for Operation Pegasus/Lam Son 207. The 1st Cavalry Division (Air Mobile) landed ten miles from Khe Sanh on 1 April 1968; they joined other American and ARVN forces to open Route 9. Elements of the Air Mobile entered Khe Sanh largely unopposed six days later. Fighting was to continue, but in effect the seventy-seven-day siege was over.

A US/ARVN force occupied Lang Vei on 10 April and a seesaw battle for its possession lasted until the 17th when the Americans finally abandoned it. On 15 April the NVA resumed its troublesome bombardment of Khe Sanh. The NVA 304th Division, recovering from its treatment by the marines in March, triggered the battle of Foxtrot Ridge following attacks on Route 9 west of Khe Sanh. To protect the road 100 marines were placed on the nearby ridge and in the early hours of 28 May an NVA battalion attacked them. For nearly nine hours the NVA pressed home their attacks but were finally driven off, suffering 230 dead; the marines lost thirteen killed and forty-four wounded. Two subsequent battles resulted in another 140 NVA dead.

Military clear-up activity in the area continued well into the following year. Operation Scotland II ran until February 1969 and resulted in over 3,000 enemy casualties around Khe Sanh. The base itself was evacuated in mid-1968 and was temporarily recaptured by the ARVN in 1971. After that it remained in NVA hands and by 1973 the airstrip had been turned into an all-weather MiG fighter runway.

Tactically the attack on Khe Sanh in 1968 was a success for North Vietnam; strategically, though, Tet in general was a disaster for the NVA/VC, with more than half the 80,000 men committed being killed. The net result was that it would take another seven years before the North would secure its long-sought-after victory over the South.

The NVA/VC underestimated the improved quality of the ARVN, who bore the brunt of the initial attacks. Once the Tet Offensive was underway it was only a matter of time before the NVA/VC forces were overwhelmed by the Americans' and South Vietnamese's superior firepower. Ground-attack aircraft and air mobility helped turn the tide. Giap blamed poor communications and co-ordination between the communist forces.

The assault on Khe Sanh and the hinterlands before and during Tet were designed to draw American forces away from the South's urban areas. Although the siege was just a feint, instead of withdrawing, the Americans took up the gauntlet. In many ways the NVA divisions committed to Khe San would have been better utilised in the battle for the cities, particularly Saigon and Hue. Both the Americans and North Vietnamese seemed to hope that Khe Sanh would prove decisive.

Nonetheless, the Dien Bien Phu comparison is not an accurate reflection of what transpired. In 1954 the French Army was trapped in a valley with little artillery and armour support, whereas the Americans had very extensive fire support inside and outside the Khe Sanh perimeter. American artillery fired almost 160,000 rounds during the siege.

The French had also lacked significant air support, whilst the US was able to call on helicopters and transport aircraft for supplies as well as ground-attack aircraft and strategic bombers to deliver heavy ordnance. For example, over 100 million pounds of napalm was dropped in the surrounding area. The Viet Minh surrounded the French with 105mm guns and 37mm anti-aircraft guns, which thwarted the resupply flights. To make matters worse, up to 30 per cent of the supplies dropped for the French garrison fell into communist hands.

The ratio of casualties also highlights a difference with Dien Bien Phu: in 1954 losses were 8,000 communists to 2,000 Frenchmen; in 1968 they were 10,000 communists to 500 Americans. According to the North Vietnamese up to 90 per cent of the NVA/VC losses were due to bombing and artillery fire.

This Huey is dropping down amongst the trees; this was not something that could be done in a 'hot' LZ.

Tet demonstrated the lack of widespread support in the South for the NVA/VC and reinforced the South Vietnamese government's claim that it was winning the war and the hearts and minds of the people. Crucially, it showed that although the guerrillas could continue to hold the countryside, US and ARVN troops were more than capable of defeating the communists whenever they could be drawn into conventional battles.

In the aftermath of Tet the communist leadership issued a directive to all its military units: 'Never again and under no circumstances are we going to risk our entire military force for just such an offensive. On the contrary, we should endeavour to preserve our military potential for future campaigns.'

Ultimately the Tet Offensive resulted in so much death and destruction that it was hard to see any real winner. While America declared Khe Sanh and Tet an overwhelming victory, it was in reality a draw. American and ARVN forces won on the battlefield, but the offensive highlighted the determination, extensive reach and capabilities of the NVA/VC. Although Giap's military was severely mauled, he did achieve a Dien Bien Phu style goal, in that world opinion was increasingly against the war and the American public were clamouring for the troops to come home.

This man is cleaning his M16, a gun that was prone to stoppages.

This shark-mouth F-4E Phantom II belongs to the 469th Tactical Fighter Squadron, with the 388th Tactical Fighter Wing flying out of Korat Royal Thai Air Force Base. This type of aircraft introduced the internal gun: the nose-mounted 20mm M61A cannon, which was useful for close-in work against enemy MiGs. For anti-MiG escort operations, weaponry also included four AIM-7 Sparrow missiles beneath the fuselage and four AIM-9 Sidewinders on wing pylons.

The NVA's SA-2 SAMs did not prove as deadly as might have been expected.

Air Cavalry to the rescue – a month after the Tet Offensive was thwarted the US 1st Cavalry Division (Air Mobile) was sent to lift the seventy-seven-day siege of Khe Sanh under Operation Pegasus.

Hueys en route to their landing zone followed by a dust off once the men were on the ground.

Securing an LZ was often a laborious job. The men in the bottom image are using a rather rickety bamboo bridge.

In March 1968 the 1st Cavalry Division shifted forces to Landing Zone Stud, the staging area for Operation Pegasus to break the siege of Khe Sanh. This long-range patrol team from Easy Company, 52nd Infantry (LRP) assigned to 1st Cavalry Division was photographed at LZ Stud on 17 April 1968. Operation Pegasus/Lam Son 207 had ended three days earlier. These men are wearing a mixture of tiger-stripe and leaf-pattern camouflage.

Men of Easy Company, 52nd Infantry, 1st Cavalry Division in Quang Tri on 26 July 1968. Most of these men are armed with the M16, but a number of them, including the man in the foreground, have been issued with the Colt Commando assault carbine.

The Huey was called on to shift all manner of supplies. In this case it is building materials – note the boards and planks.

A Huey spraying defoliant. Operation Ranch Hand led to accusations that America was conducting chemical warfare. In January 1968 the US ambassador to South Vietnam, Ellsworth Bunker, set up a herbicide review committee to assess the programme. A key economic loss was the destruction of hardwood timber in War Zones C and D. Tragically little attention was paid to the long-term effects of the poisonous dioxin in Agent Orange on humans.

In 1968, after the loss of three aircraft on the initial Combat Lancer deployment, the General Dynamics F-111 two-seat tactical strike fighter was withdrawn and did not return for four years.

Regular Convair F-102A Delta Dagger deployments were made to Tan Son Nhut and Da Nang. Initially they were sent to South Vietnam for air defence, but they also flew escort for B-52s, flying against targets in the North Vietnamese panhandle. On such a mission one F-102A was lost on 3 February 1968 to a MiG-21. These three-tone camouflaged aircraft were photographed over Thailand.

Chapter Eleven

Battle Won, War Lost

Thanks to the US media coverage of the Tet Offensive the North Vietnamese quickly realised that they had a massive propaganda victory on their hands. Nonetheless, there were recriminations in Hanoi about what went wrong. Those senior leaders within the North Vietnamese communist party who had advocated a swift victory through a mixture of conventional offensive and widespread guerrilla uprising found themselves roundly discredited. Critics argued that it was simply too much too soon.

The leadership's major failure was to underestimate the mobility of American and South Vietnamese forces. In addition the Tet Offensive was vastly ambitious and meant that once US forces and the ARVN had recovered, they were able to crush the communist attacks piecemeal.

The NVA's General Tran Van Tra admitted as much, saying, 'We did not correctly evaluate the specific balance of forces between ourselves and the enemy, did not fully realize that the enemy still had considerable capabilities, and that our capabilities were limited, and set requirements that were beyond our actual strength.'

General Tran Do, North Vietnamese commander at the battle of Hue, recognised that their defeat in fact had a silver lining: 'In all honesty, we didn't achieve our main objective, which was to spur uprisings throughout the South. Still, we inflicted heavy casualties on the Americans and their puppets, and this was a big gain for us. As for making an impact in the United States, it had not been our intention – but it turned out to be a fortunate result.'

The leadership in South Vietnam was traumatised by the whole affair and realised too late that the ARVN was not up to the job of protecting them from the combined efforts of the NVA and VC. As a result the government moved to mobilise 200,000 extra troops. Previous attempts to do this had been thwarted by political opposition, but this time the South Vietnamese rallied behind their government as they were appalled by the North's actions over Tet and the widespread guerrilla attacks that had targeted their homes.

Behind the scenes the South Vietnamese government was rattled by Washington's claim that the US military had been taken by surprise. Once America halted its bombing of North Vietnam and commenced negotiations with the North,

Saigon became convinced that the Americans were going to abandon them. The South began to fear peace more than war and this sentiment underscored all subsequent peace negotiations. The rot had set in and nothing could really be done to remedy it.

Tet graphically highlighted what a tenuous hold the MACV had on the situation. In fact, Tet and Khe Sanh proved to be the foundation of the American withdrawal and were a major reason that President Johnson withdrew his candidacy for re-election. This forced an administration change on the US, which in the long run was good for North Vietnam. Johnson's greatest failing was not taking a firmer stand after Tet. General Westmoreland returned to America to become Chief of Staff.

Peace talks commenced in Paris in May 1968 and the following year America began to reduce its military presence. After Tet there was a general mobilisation in South Vietnam, heralding a policy of Vietnamisation (whereby the South finally took responsibility for military operations), and 1968–72 saw a major expansion of South Vietnam's armed forces. The North Vietnamese became more cautious during 1969 because of their losses, and also due to the American process of Vietnamisation. The North was biding its time, infiltrating 115,000 men into the South to make good its losses. The bulk of the American, Australian, New Zealand, South Korean and Thai troops pulled out in the early 1970s.

In an effort to shore up the ARVN in 1972 America supplied fifty-nine tanks and 100 APCs from a depot in Japan. In the Easter offensive of 1972 the NVA used large numbers of tanks to spearhead their attacks on three separate fronts. The NVA units were the most heavily armed to ever enter South Vietnam: the attacking forces were equipped with T-34, T-54 and PT-76 tanks, along with SA-2 and SA-7 missiles and 130mm guns.

The main attack, across the northern demilitarised zone, which began on 30 March 1972, employed a total of 100 tanks. These came up against the ARVN 20th Tank Regiment, which held long enough for the ARVN to recover the situation with American air power. Those tanks that were used for attacks on Kontum and Binh Long provinces, without adequate artillery or infantry support, fell prey to ARVN anti-tank weapons. US air power again played a decisive role and the NVA lost 250 AFVs. In one engagement ARVN M48s destroyed eleven NVA tanks and from that point onwards conventional tank warfare became commonplace. Despite the peace treaty of 1973 the North kept up the military pressure and the ARVN disintegrated in 1975.

For a long time the USAF had complete control of the skies over South-east Asia. In total the USAF claimed 137 MiG kills. Nevertheless, by 1972, once the North Vietnamese Army became equipped with shoulder-launched SAM-7 and radar-controlled AAA, all but the most modern aircraft became obsolescent. It also restricted low-flying and helicopter operations. In December 1972 the North fired 1,242 surface-to-air missiles at the USAF, exhausting their defences and leaving the Americans free to roam at will. The Americans did not have everything their own way – during Operation Linebacker II they lost twenty-six aircraft, including fifteen B-52s. Also within two years the North had recovered its strength.

This effectively neutralised South Vietnam's air superiority and by 1975 the North Vietnamese Army was superior in both weaponry and supplies, thus giving the North the technological edge. This was a decisive factor in the final offensive after the US military – and in particular its air cover – had been withdrawn. Equipped mainly with twin-jet-engine Cessna A-37 Dragonflys, the South Vietnamese Air Force was simply not fast enough at low altitude and could not save its crumbling army in 1975.

Also by 1975 the NVA had some 600 Russian T-54 and Chinese Type 59 medium tanks. The NVA had learned their lesson from three years earlier, training for combined-arms operations. There was no stopping the NVA using sudden assault and deep advance tactics. By then ARVN armoured units had been debilitated due to shortages of ammunition and spares, and under such conditions they were unable to stem the enemy armour.

Advancing 50km a day, within two months they were in striking distance of Saigon. Shorn of American air cover the South collapsed. On 30 April 1975 four NVA armoured columns converged on the city driving on Doc Lap Palace where T-54s clashed with M41s for one last time. Saigon had fallen and the Vietnam War was at an end.

In June 1968 MACV Commander General Westmoreland was replaced by General Creighton Abrams. While this decision had been made the previous year, it was inevitably seen by the US media as punishment for being caught out by the Tet Offensive. In addition Westmoreland's assessment of America's appetite for the war to a joint session of Congress in 1967 proved hollow post-Tet: 'In evaluating the enemy strategy,' he said, 'it is evident to me that he believes our Achilles heel is our resolve. . . . Your continued strong support is vital to the success of our mission. . . . Backed at home by resolve, confidence, patience, determination, and continued support, we will prevail in Vietnam over the communist aggressor!' This was no sacking, though, as Westmoreland served as Chief of Staff of the US Army from 1968 to 1972.

During the evacuation operations of 28/29 April 1975 so many South Vietnamese Air Force helicopters flew to the amphibious command ship USS *Blue Ridge* that many had to be pushed overboard. In the subsequent Sino-Vietnamese War of 1979 neither side made significant use of air power, though the Vietnamese undoubtedly made some use of their Hueys, quantities of which had been seized at Tan Son Nhut air base.

A US Navy McDonnell F-4B Phantom II of Fighter Squadron VF-111 'Sundowners' dropping 227kg Mk 82 bombs over Vietnam during 1971. VF-111 was assigned to Attack Carrier Air Wing 15 (CVW-15) aboard the aircraft carrier USS *Coral Sea* for a deployment to Vietnam from 12 November 1971 to 17 July 1972.

A knocked-out NVA ZSU-57 self-propelled anti-aircraft gun. In 1968 America lost 1,669 fixed-wing aircaft and helicopters: this was an all-time high for the entire war and the majority were claimed by anti-aircraft artillery and small arms.

Vietnamese porters on the vital Ho Chi Minh trail. Although named by the Americans after the North Vietnamese president the communists called it the Truong Song strategic supply route, after the Vietnamese name for the Annamite mountain range in central Vietnam. Ironically most of the trail was located in neighbouring Laos. It was never successfully cut despite all the American airpower and technology thrown at it. In 1968 over 81,000 tons of supplies were moved down it to support the forces committed to the Tet Offensive – effectively over a ton for every man involved.

A Vietnamese bridge brought down by the USAF – ultimately such actions failed to stem the communist tide.

NVA vehicles making their way through the jungle. The NVA got ever bolder in the use of tanks.

ARVN soldiers on a Chinese-supplied NVA Type 59 tank that was captured during the North's 1972 Easter offensive. North Vietnam ended up with about 350 of these tanks.

NVA heavy artillery firing on ARVN targets in 1972.

Flying under radar control with a B-66 Destroyer, USAF F-105 Thunderchiefs bomb a military target through low clouds over the southern panhandle of North Vietnam. In the years after the Tet Offensive, despite America's relentless bombing of the North and the communist lines of communication in South Vietnam's neigbours, Saigon remained effectively under siege.

A North Vietnamese Army regular. The NVA attempted to seize South Vietnam with conventional assaults in 1968 and 1972 – both ended in defeat. The third attempt in 1975 was successful, but by then a demoralised ARVN had all but collapsed.

A Cambodian fighter armed with an AK-47 – as feared, the Vietnam War spilled over into neighbouring Cambodia and Laos, where the Khmer Rouge and the Pathet Lao fought to take over their respective countries.

Communist troops storm through Tan Son Nhut air base in 1975 – behind them are abandoned C-7A Caribou and C-47 Skytrain transport aircraft, both of which had been instrumental at Khe Sanh.

Seven long years after the Tet Offensive NVA tanks finally rolled into Saigon, bringing an end to the Vietnam War.

The fate of many of the ARVN and VNAF helicopters after fleeing the NVA invasion in 1975.

Epilogue

General Giap, always lauded as one of the key architects of the Tet Offensive, lived to the ripe old age of 102, dying on 4 October 2013. After the Vietnam War he remained minister of defence and became deputy prime minister in 1976, serving until 1991. In the years since, research has suggested that Giap was in fact against the offensive and that, as he was visiting Budapest for medical treatment at the time, had little direct control over the campaign. Certainly he did not return until after the offensive had commenced, which was overseen by his Chief of Staff General Van Tien Dung and Ho Chi Minh's right-hand man, the politician Le Duan.

In the opinion of the American public the Viet Cong in their black pyjamas, rubber sandals and straw coolie hats had humbled the US Army, US Marine Corps and the ARVN during the Tet Offensive. In reality the VC had been bolstered by whole divisions of the North Vietnamese Army, equipped with heavy artillery, anti-aircraft guns and surface-to-air missiles, and supported by MiG jet fighters. The conventional Tet Offensive achieved little but to exhaust the NVA and VC, forcing them to resume guerrilla warfare. Nonetheless, the popular perception was set that the US military had won a pyrrhic victory over men in pyjamas armed with little more than rifles. Many argued that such dogged determination could be not be overcome and this sentiment sapped the political and military will to prosecute the Vietnam War to a successful outcome. From 1968 onwards America was considering its exit options.

Following the fall of Saigon in 1975, alarm that the whole of Indochina would fall under communist rule proved to be justified. Tet signalled the high-water mark of US military power in the region and it was all downhill from then on. In the wake of America's withdrawal from South Vietnam and the public humiliation of US foreign policy, Washington became highly risk averse. America's fears of a domino effect in South-east Asia were immediately realised as communist forces took power in Cambodia and Laos – only Thailand was spared. America was to take little comfort at the region's communist parties turning on each other.

Ironically the Khmer Rouge communist party in Cambodia was created in 1968 as an offshoot of the North Vietnamese Army. With the backing of North Vietnam they eventually seized power in 1975, while the communist Pathet Lao in neighbouring Laos took power at the same time. From then on America stayed its hand with major military adventures until the 1980s when is flexed its military muscles over Grenada and Lebanon. However, it was not until 1991 and the Gulf War that US military pride was fully restored.

Ironically, unified Vietnam rapidly fell out with its Tet allies. Vietnam's communists and those in neighbouring Cambodia once had common cause but this soon dissipated. Border clashes with the Khmer Rouge led to a Vietnamese invasion of Cambodia in 1978, which then put Vietnam at loggerheads with China. The following year China invaded Vietnam due to a row over Vietnam's treatment of its Chinese minority and the Spratly Islands. There was little the Soviet Union could do and it stood back as 200,000 Chinese troops poured across the Vietnamese border. Vietnam was forced to redeploy its forces in Cambodia. The three-week war was short lived, though heavy fighting took place at Lang Son; having made its point, China subsequently withdrew. These inter-communist conflicts were seen as little more than footnotes to the greater conflagration that was the Vietnam War – after all, it is the Tet Offensive that everyone remembers as the classic example of how to win the battle but lose the war.

Suggested Further Reading

Anderson, Christopher J., *Marines in Vietnam,* Greenhill Books, London, 2002.

Arnold, James R., *The Illustrated History of The Vietnam War: Armor*, Bantam Books, New York, 1987.

Berry, F. Clifton, Jr, *The Illustrated History of The Vietnam War: Gadget Warfare*, Bantam Books, New York, 1988.

Bonds, Ray (ed.), *The Vietnam War: The Illustrated History of the Conflict in Southeast Asia*, Salamander, London, 1981.

Cawthorne, Nigel, *Vietnam: A War Lost and Won,* Arcturus Publishing, London, 2003.

Collins, J.L., Jr. *The Development and Training of the South Vietnamese Army, 1950–1972*, Dept of the Army, Washington, DC, 1975.

Dorr, Robert F., *Air War South Vietnam*, Arms and Armour Press, London, 1990.

Dunstan, Simon, *Armour of the Vietnam Wars*, Osprey Publishing, London, 1985.

Francillon, René J., *Vietnam Air Wars*, Guild Publishing, London, 1987.

Karnow, Stanley, *Vietnam, A History: The First Complete Account of Vietnam at War,* Penguin, Harmondsworth, 1984.

Katcher, Philip, *Armies of the Vietnam War, 1962–75*, Osprey Publishing, London, 1980.

O'Balance, Edgar, *The Wars in Vietnam, 1954–73*, Ian Allan, Shepperton, 1975.

Robinson, Anthony (ed.), *Weapons of the Vietnam War*, Bison Books, London, 1983.

Russell, Lee E., *Armies of the Vietnam War (2)*, Osprey Publishing, London, 1983.

Starry, General Donn A., *Armoured Combat in Vietnam,* Blandford Press, Poole, 1981.

Thompson, Leroy, *Uniforms of the Indo-China and Vietnam Wars,* Blandford Press, Poole, 1984.

Welsh, Douglas, *The History of the Vietnam War,* Bison Books, London, 1981.

Welsh, Douglas, *The Vietnam War,* Bison Books, London, 1982.

White, Justin, *The Viet Nam Wars,* Weidenfeld and Nicolson, London, 1991.

Woodruff, M.W., *Unheralded Victory: Who Won the Vietnam War,* Collins, London, 2000.